THE INFLUENCE

OF SPIRITUAL BEINGS

UPON MAN

RUDOLF STEINER

Eleven Lectures delivered in Berlin
between January 6 and June 11, 1908

1961

ANTHROPOSOPHIC PRESS, INC.

NEW YORK

Translated from shorthand reports
unrevised by the lecturer

This translation has been authorized for
the western hemisphere by agreement with
the Rudolf Steiner Nachlassverwaltung,
Dornach, Switzerland.
The original edition was issued under the
title:
*Das Hereinwirken geistiger Wesenheiten
in den Menschen.*

PRINTED IN THE UNITED STATES OF AMERICA

In his autobiography, *THE COURSE OF MY LIFE* (chapters 35 and 36), Rudolf Steiner speaks as follows concerning the character of this privately printed matter:

"The content of this printed matter was intended as oral communications, not to be printed. . . . ,

"Nothing has ever been said that is not in utmost degree the purest result of the developing Anthroposophy. . . . Whoever reads this privately printed material can take it in the fullest sense as containing what Anthroposophy has to say. Therefore it was possible without hesitation . . . to depart from the plan of circulating this printed matter among members alone. Only, it will be necessary to put up with the fact that erroneous matter is included in the lecture reports which I did not revise.

"The right to a judgment about the content of such privately printed material can naturally be conceded only to one who knows what is taken for granted as the prerequisite basis of this judgment. And for most of this printed matter prerequisite will be *at least* the Anthroposophical knowledge of the human being, and of the cosmos, to the extent that their nature is set forth in Anthroposophy, and of what exists in the form of 'Anthroposophical history' in the communications from the world of spirit."

CONTENTS

vii

between the inner soul nature and these spiritual
beings man can grasp the space forces which
take the form of architecture for the physical
body, as well as the form forces which take the
form of sculpture for the etheric body, painting
for the sentient soul. The harmonies of the
spheres take the form of music for the intellectual soul. The words of the spiritual world
which the consciousness soul receives in the
night take the form of poetry in the day consciousness. Richard Wagner and his relation to
art. His attempt to unite Shakespeare and
Beethoven. Glance into future times when all
external things in man's surroundings (e.g railway stations, and so forth), will again be image
of the spiritual reality. The mission of Spiritual
Science in the evolution of mankind. . . June
11, 1908   175

*Note regarding Rudolf Steiner's use of the word
"Theosophy":*
The word "Theosophy" refers in every instance
to the independent Spiritual Science founded by
Rudolf Steiner, as presented in his book *THE-
OSOPHY,* and other works.   Editor.

I

TODAY we shall have to speak from the aspect of Spiritual Science about various facts and beings of the higher worlds and about their connection with man. It must be pointed out from the outset, although in such a working group it might seem unnecessary, that today's lecture is intended for those students of spiritual matters who have reached a more advanced stage. This must be possible from time to time. One who is a newcomer at these Monday lectures may perhaps feel somewhat surprised by what is said today, yet we should make no progress if we did not sometimes discuss things pertaining to the higher spheres of spiritual science. It is possible that someone who has only lately met the truths of Spiritual Science and is waiting to be convinced may find a sort of craziness in many things to be expressed today, but such provinces must be touched upon from time to time.

You will have gathered from the lectures given here recently that when we ascend with clairvoyance into the higher worlds we there meet with beings who, it is true, do not belong to our physical world, but who are in themselves so independent that we can describe them as 'persons' for those worlds, just as we call men here on the physical plane 'persons.' You have seen that groups of animals of the same species together belong to a group-soul or group-ego and that on the astral plane we come upon the lion-soul, the tiger-soul, and so on, as independent personalities whom we can meet there as we meet the human being on the physical plane. In the same way we find in still higher regions, on the devachanic plane, the egos of quite large plant groups, and in the highest parts of Devachan we find the egos of the minerals, personalities as distinct as men are here on the physical plane. We saw in this way that in these higher worlds we meet with certain beings who, so to speak, extend part of their organism, their separate members, down into the physical plane. If a man were to extend his fingers through openings in a curtain or partition we should only see the ten fingers, the man himself would be behind the partition. So it is with the group-egos of the animals. Here with the physical eye we see what is extended down below as members by higher beings of the astral world, and the actual ego is behind the partition, behind that wall which separates the physical world from the astral world. And in a corresponding way this holds good for the other group-egos, the group-egos of the plant or the mineral world. When we raise ourselves from the physical world into higher worlds we meet not only these beings who have been described as extending their members down below here, but we meet a whole number of other beings who may equally well be considered personalities for those worlds, but whose physical members are not so directly visible and evident as those of the group egos of animals, plants, and minerals.

The astral plane and devachanic plane are in fact densely populated worlds. We find many kinds of beings there whose effects are manifested here on the physical plane though not obviously, and who have much to do with the physical plane, with our whole modern human life. One does not understand this life if one does not know that beings who live above in higher worlds are active within it. In the human body itself much goes on over which man is not master, which is not the expression of the human ego but the deed, effect, manifestation, of beings of higher worlds. It is of these things that we will speak today.

When we observe the astral plane we come upon certain beings there—only one kind among many—who seem to have no expression or manifestation among the beings found on the physical plane, but who are yet connected with it. There on the astral plane we meet with them as astral beings—with pronounced will, pronounced purposes, and so on. Within our immediate world they have this existence on the astral plane, but they are related, belong, to the same sort of beings as inhabit our present moon, having even a certain physical existence on the moon. One who is able to approach these things clairvoyantly knows that on their scene of action, the moon, these are beings in a certain respect similar to man, but that they are dwarfs in comparison, scarcely reaching the height of a six or seven year old child. Upon the moon, however, a particular opportunity is offered them for their activity. The physical conditions are quite different there, the atmosphere for instance is quite different and in consequence when these beings withdraw, so to speak, to their habitat they acquire the faculty of a tremendous roaring, of uttering immensely powerful, frightful sounds. These dwarf-like beings can maintain an astral existence within our world. You must in fact picture conditions in the higher worlds as being much more complicated than people are wont to do.

As soon as we speak from the aspect of the higher worlds, there exists an unbroken connection between the different planets and so the moon is connected with the earth just as for instance Berlin and Hamburg are connected by the telephone. Beings that live on the moon can therefore carry out

3

their operations on the earth with the aid of astral forces. One might call them the reverse side of other beings whom we also find in the astral world, beneficent beings who, compared even with the mildest human nature, are yet much, much milder—in their speech too, very mild and gentle. The speech of these beings has not that aridity of human language which a man must ponder over a long time if he is to express himself, and clothe his thoughts and ideas in words. One could say that the thoughts of these beings flow from their lips—not merely the expression of the thoughts in words, but thoughts themselves flow in a gentle language from their lips. These beings are likewise to be found within our astral world; they have their actual scene of action on another planet. As the first-named beings are at home on the moon, these second are at home on Mars, they inhabit Mars and are in fact the main population—as certain human races are the principal population on our earth. If we then mount up higher to the devachanic plane we find certain beings who in their own way are also of a mild, peaceable nature and who in a certain respect are extraordinarily clever. These beings to be found on the devachanic plane have their actual home on the planet Venus, as the other beings on moon and Mars. On Venus too we find yet a second species of beings who—in contrast to the gentle, amiable kind—present a wild and furious vitality, and whose principal occupation consists in mutual fighting and plunder.

Again we find on the higher parts of the devachanic plane certain beings who are very difficult to describe. We can only do so comparatively by saying that they are infinitely inventive: at every moment of life they devise something—for it would be false to say that they think it out. Their inventive gift is rather as if one were to look at something and at the same instant—even in the beholding—one had the

4

impression of how one could form it differently. Invention comes to them spontaneously. These beings, who have their home on Saturn, are again confronted by others who seem to be their reverse side; savage, horrible beings who possess to an infinitely higher, more frightful degree all that lives in man as wild, sensual greed and inordinate desire.

Now all these beings who have been mentioned are by no means unconnected with our existence. Their deeds, activities, manifestations, are definitely extended into our life and their action is particularly to be traced by clairvoyance when certain conditions appear on earth. Thus the beings who—naturally as astral beings—are at home on the moon are present on earth in the most varied circumstances, when for instance a man falls a prey to illusionary ideas, or where insane people are gathered. Such astral beings show special preference for the neighborhood of insane asylums. They are, moreover, almost always to be found near mediums and somnambulists; these persons have such beings swirling round them, and a large proportion of the influences that are exercised upon them is derived from the presence of these creatures. Where on the other hand love and kindliness prevail, where humanitarianism is unfolded, there you find the mild, gentle Mars beings present as astral creations, taking part in the forces which are there at work. That is nourishment for them, the atmosphere in which they can live and whence they exercise their influence on man.

Whenever human discoveries are made, where engineers are at work, in technical workshops, there the atmosphere is created for the inventive Saturn beings. On the other hand where some sort of activity is developed which has to do with presence of mind, beings are there who have their seat on Venus.

So you see how man in the most varied circumstances is

5

continually accompanied by such swirling elemental beings, as they may be called. Man is really never alone; whatever he does and whatever he undertakes is at the same time an opportunity for the development of a number of beings. Man's deeds, both fine and crude, deeds of idealism and the most ugly deeds, all give an opportunity for the presence of creatures who encroach into man's forces and occupy themselves there and whom one must know if one is to get a true view of life. He who does not realize these things passes through life in complete blindness. We are not concerned here with mere theory or a theoretical challenge; all these things are directly practical. For man will only little by little in the future earthly evolution learn to act and frame his conduct on right lines, when he begins to recognize what creatures are summoned in response to certain deeds and circumstances. Everything that man does is like a summons to unknown beings. It is not only the insane or mediums that these moon beings—among whom are thoroughly malevolent little rascals, can venture to approach; when, for instance, young children are overfed in such a senseless way that they become greedy, then these beings can sidle up to them and spoil their development. You see then how necessary it is for man to know what he stirs up around him through his behavior and whole attitude in the world!

Now these beings in yet another respect are by no means unconnected with man. They have on the contrary a deep relation to our human structure. Of all that exists in the human body, there is actually only one thing that belongs or can increasingly belong to man—and that is his blood. Man's blood is the direct expression of his ego. If however he is not perpetually careful to strengthen his ego inwardly through a strong and vigorous will, through strong forces of his soul, if so to speak, he loses control of his ego then

6

other beings can fasten upon his blood, and that is very grave and evil for him. On the other hand, many other beings are anchored in other parts of the present human organism. We will now see all that actually stretches its feelers into the human body, all that is anchored there. But we must first examine the human body a little.

You are aware that the blood as it flows through the arteries and spreads out in the body is the expression of man's ego and that it becomes a stronger and stronger expression as the ego itself finds its centre, finds its inner centre of strength in an increasing degree. Man's ego will only in a far distant future obtain control of other enclosed portions of the organism. Many other beings are still contained today in these other constituents of the human body. Let us call to mind, for example, the three bodily humors, the three juices, chyle, lymph, blood, in order to study them more closely. You perhaps know the significance that these three kinds of fluid have for man. You know that when food is taken in, it is first conveyed through the preparatory organs into the stomach, mixed and prepared with the right juices secreted by the glands so that it can be worked upon through the intestines. There the food is brought into a pulpy condition, the chyme, which is conveyed forwards through the intestines. Whatever can form nutritious material for man is then passed into the body through minute vascular organs called the 'villi,' in order to serve as nutritive juices for renewing the body. This is one of the substances which we have in the body and which we call the 'chyle.'

Then perhaps you also know that besides the chyle, which is produced through the entry into the human body of food from outside, there are other vessels inside the body of a similar nature which conduct a species of fluid resembling in a certain respect the white substance in our blood.

This juice flows through the whole human organism in certain vessels which very largely take the same course as the blood vessels we call veins, because they contain blue-red blood. These even take up the chyle too. The fluid which they contain is the lymph. This is a juice which one might say is spiritualized in comparison with the uniform food juice, the chyle. The vessels which convey the lymph take their course throughout the whole body, in a certain respect they even pass through the bone marrow and what they convey then absorbs the chyle too. All the lymph which is spread out and runs through the left half of the body and lower extremities—that is the left side of the head, left side of the trunk, the left hand and both legs—all this is collected, flows into the left clavicular vein and then empties into the blood circulation. Only the lymph contained in vessels on the right side of the head and the right side of the trunk, unite and enter the right clavicular vein so that in this way the lymph vessels become the expression of an important fact.

You see how man is divided into two parts; not, indeed, symmetrically, but so that one part comprises all the lower parts of the body with the left half of the trunk and head, while the other part is formed from the right side of the trunk and head. Lymph is a second fluid pulsating in man, a fluid that stands much nearer to the soul than does the chyle, the gastric and intestinal juices of the chyle. It is true that the digestion and the whole circulation of the chyle are also influenced greatly by the soul conditions, but these are much more deeply connected with the lymph. In a man who is very active and energetic the lymph flows much more vigorously than in a man who is heavy, lazy and inactive. We could instance many conditions of the soul

8

which are connected with the course of the lymph in the human body.

The third fluid is the blood, of which we have often spoken. It comprises a red life-giving blood, rich in oxygen that flows in the arteries and a blue-red blood rich in carbon that flows in the veins. And as our blood is the expression of our ego, so is the lymph in a certain direction the expression of the human astral body. Such things do not manifest themselves merely in *one* direction. From another aspect the nerve-system is the expression of the astral body. To-day we will consider the aspect in which the deed, the revelation, the expression, of the astral body is the lymph. Just as a man can fill two professions so too can the astral body be on the one hand the builder of the nerve-system, and on the other hand the builder, the creator, of the lymph. In the same way man's etheric body is the builder and creator of the whole glandular system, as well as in another aspect the organizer, creator, and controller of the circulation of the chyle. Here you have the connection of these fluids taking their course in the human body, with the members of human nature itself.

Now we must be clear that in the human astral body and etheric body, the ego is definitely not the only master. Gradually in the course of evolution man's ego attains to a greater control over his astral body and his etheric body as he changes the former into spirit-self or Manas and the latter into life spirit or Budhi. But as long as man has not control of these parts of his being, other beings are connected with these human members.

In the human astral body other beings are embedded like the maggots in cheese—forgive the unappetizing comparison—but so it is. And in fact the astral beings which are embedded in, and connected with, the human astral body are

9

those whom I have described as having their real habitat on the moon or Mars, according as they are benevolent or malevolent. They anchor themselves there. And lymph, the whitish juice that courses through man, belongs to the body of beings who live in our astral world. To be sure, these beings of the astral plane, with their real home on the moon or Mars, are not so obvious as are the animal group-egos. But they are of such an astral nature that in a certain other direction we can say: just as in an animal group, a group of lions, for instance, we have a kind of manifestation of the distinct personality on the astral plane, the lion-ego, so in the lymph passing through the human body we have, though not so obviously, the manifestation, the extended members, of these astral beings.

Then—you may ask—have these astral beings as much a kind of physical existence as the group-souls of the animals, as the group-ego of the Lion-species in its manifestation in the single lions here on the physical plane? If you ask this question, one would have to answer: yes, they have. Just as in the case of the animals we saw that the astral group-ego extends its separate members into the separate lion-individuals, so these astral beings also extend their physical being here. They could not, however, extend it from outside into the physical plane; for this they need beings on the physical plane whose parasites they are, into whom they fasten and bore. They are here the parasites of men. If there were no human race here on earth they would very soon take their departure, they could find no dwelling place, it would not suit them here. But there are beings, men and higher animals, who have lymph and there these beings have their physical manifestation. Thus not merely a material substance pulses through our body but in such circulation move whole hosts of these beings. They revolve through man, move along through him and have their bodies in the lymph—whereas the actual human being, the ego-man has his body, to begin with, merely in the blood. And the preponderance of moon beings or Mars beings of this nature circling through a man gives his lymph its special character. If more moon beings circulate through his body he is a man who inclines more easily to wrong-doing, irritation, and anger, if more Mars beings, then he is a man who is more inclined to gentleness, kindliness, mildness. You see how man is not traversed merely by fluids but also by spirits, and how one only understands man when one knows that spirits pass through him and not fluids merely.

Now if you examine clairvoyantly what one calls chyle, that is, the external expression of the human etheric body, you find that similar beings are also incorporated into this. The beings primarily anchored there are those whom we have already characterized as the good and the evil Venus beings, those having their home on Venus and existing in our devachanic world. There they are personalities for clairvoyant vision and they have their expression, their manifestation, here in physical life in the human chyle— however strange that may seem. Living in this fluid that courses through the human body, these beings have their actual home on the devachanic plane, and in so far as they take on a physical body, have their physical life on Venus. And since Venus is connected in a certain way through its forces with our whole earthly vegetation and all that lives on earth, you will realize the connection existing between man's nourishment and the effect produced in him through what he takes in as nourishment. That most assuredly is not a matter of indifference. Influences of the Venus beings live in all the plants and naturally also in the animal kingdom. The influences may come on the one hand from the good, gentle, mild Venus beings, or on the other hand, from the wild beings who have been described to you as greedy for plunder and engaged in conflict with each other. According as the one or the other kind work upon our animals and plants, so are virtues or vices built into man's body when the flesh of these animals or the food obtained from these plants are transformed into the chyle.

By this you can see, from a higher standpoint than could be presented in earlier lectures, how important it is to know about human nutrition from the aspect of spiritual science, to know the influences under which the various plants and animals are standing. You can gather, for instance, that one who knows that plants and animals standing under certain celestial influences flourish in a certain country, can also learn to grasp how a quite definite national character must arise. For in everything that man consumes from his environment he eats, not only the substances analyzed by chemistry, he eats at the same time definite spirits, and it is these spirits which enter through his mouth into the stomach and spread out through his being. There the perspective opens to us of how the character of a people can be known from the deeper geographical constitution of a country.

Do not forget a remark which you can find in the lecture on *the Lord's Prayer** where such a fact was presented from quite a different aspect. There it was stated that man stands in a certain relation to his whole people through his etheric body, and is connected through his astral body with his nearer surroundings.

Here again you see illuminated from a still deeper aspect how folk-character is formed from the spiritual beings which are absorbed into man with his food. It is one of the means by which the great spiritual guidance of the earth distributes

* Rudolf Steiner, *The Lord's Prayer*, Anthroposophic Press, New York.

the different national characters over the earth; foods which produce one or another effect have been distributed in such a way that the character of a certain people arises from the nourishment that it obtains. That does not lead in a round-about way to materialism: spiritual science shows how everything of a material nature is a revelation of the spirit and how in a way unknown to man spiritual influences are themselves diffused within him.

It is more difficult to understand the way in which the Saturn spirits work upon man. There are on the one hand Saturn spirits who directly they observe anything immediately make some invention, on the other hand there are those who develop terribly disordered passions of a sensual nature, in comparison with which all that man can develop in this direction is child's play. These Saturn spirits insinuate themselves into the human body in a still more hidden way, namely, through sense perception. When we turn our eye to a beautiful, pure and noble thing, a concept is aroused in us; when we turn our eye to a sordid, ignoble thing then a different concept is aroused. Now when a concept is called forth in the soul through outer impressions there slip into man at the same time these Saturn spirits—the good and the bad. And through all that man by his mere sympathies and antipathies unfolds around himself as environment, as what he hears and sees and smells, he exposes himself to the insinuations of the one or other order of the Saturn-spirits. When man is sensing they draw into him through eyes and ears and the whole skin. It is quite frightful, for instance, to observe occultly what dissolute spirits insinuate themselves into the nose of persons out of their surroundings, through many perfumes that are highly prized in human society—quite apart from what slinks into the nose of those who carry these perfumes on their own person.

We see from this how finely and closely one must observe the most everyday things from the spiritual standpoint if one wants to be clear about life. Much could be told you of people who more or less consciously knew how to command spirits which particularly work upon man through scents and slip into him with the perfume. If you had a deeper, more intimate knowledge of various things in history, particularly the history of France at the time of Louis XIII, XIV, and XV, with all the arts developed there, where in fact aromas played an important part in the drama of intrigue, you would then have an idea of what men are able to do—consciously or unconsciously—who know how to command the spirits which creep into human sense perception in perfumes. I could refer you to quite an attractive book* that has been written recently by the Minister of a little Court. He wrote it naturally without any knowledge of these facts, but he was quite clear about the effects. It is a very interesting book about this little Court where a notable catastrophe took place in recent years, and where the Minister and dignitary concerned describes from his Memoirs the machinations of a person** who in a certain way knew how to command aromas and their spirits. And he describes it with a certain satisfaction because he was armed against it and had not fallen a victim. You see, these things are not without significance and effect for practical life. When one understands life not as a blind materialist, but as a seeing man, then one can trace the spiritual influences everywhere —and if the influences are known, life is understood for the first time.

So you see how we must picture man to ourselves as quite

* Dr. Vladan Georgevitch: *Das Ende der Obrenovitch* (Leipzig, 1905).
** Draga Maschin, who was murdered with Alexander I of Serbia at Belgrade on June 11, 1903.

, complicated being, as an associate of many kinds of worlds, many kinds of beings. One who advances on the path of occult development to ever higher stages of knowledge learns to know these beings in their special nature and thereby becomes independent of them, he is able to view them from an independent standpoint. To take into oneself the truth concerning higher worlds means to become really free, really mature, for we are then aware of the activities and impulses which pulse and flow through our life. Learning to know one's way means at the same time to become free and independent.

And just as one can point to certain fluids pulsing through man, so can certain human organs be indicated in which beings of the higher worlds likewise find their expression and manifestation. Thus, for instance, the beings just described to you as Saturn beings find their expression in a certain respect in the human liver. You must of course be clear that if one really wants to understand Spiritual Science one discovers it to be a very complicated domain.

You are aware that in the Saturn development of human evolution the first inception of the senses came into existence through the forces of Saturn. In a similar way Saturn still works into man and among his inner bodily organs it is the liver upon which the Saturn forces have a strong and intensive influence. The human being who is on the way to evolve beyond everything of a Saturn nature, must therefore grow beyond the forces which are anchored in his liver. And although certain forces are present in the liver from which man must free himself, yet they were necessary to enable him to come to his present form and shape; they must however be overcome. You can prove this in a certain way by external evidence. You can discover, for instance, that in the period before birth and directly after birth, when the

15

human body is being built up, the liver occupies the greatest space in relation to the rest of the body and that then it becomes smaller and smaller. In fact the ratio at birth could be given as 1 :18 whereas the relation later is 1 :36. The liver decreases approximately by one half, and thus by purely natural development man overcomes the forces rooted in it.

Inasmuch as earthly man is intended to evolve to higher and higher spirituality he has acquired as an outward physical expression the power to overcome the liver forces. In a certain way the lungs represent the counter-organ to the liver. They do not enclose everything egotistically in themselves as the liver does, they open man fully outwards, he stands in continual communication with the world through the air that he takes in and again gives out. A combustion goes on in the lungs. The blue-red carbon-rich blood enters the lungs and is transformed through its combination with oxygen into red life-giving blood. Just as in a burning flame the substances unite with the oxygen, so in the lungs there is a process of burning. Breathing may be called a combustion process, and with this breathing and combustion process man has been endowed with the prospect of attaining a higher and higher evolution. The forces which built him up have reached their ultimate stage in the liver. The forces which he receives like a fire from the air will rescue him from the forces chaining him to earth. The fire which man receives from the air and which is expressed in his breathing is that which leads him upwards to ever higher spheres.

Myths and legends are always deeper and more filled with wisdom than our apparently advanced science. In the Prometheus myth we have a magnificent expression of what has just been related from the facts of human life.

16

The myth says that Prometheus brought man fire from heaven and indicates in this way that Prometheus participates in the process which is expressed in the human breath and which leads man upwards. But a wonderful explanation is given: because Prometheus raises himself above the forces which chain man to the earth and opposes them, because he is the one to give man this force of the fire, therefore he must suffer for it. The suffering is wonderfully represented as the fact underlying the Myth, namely, a vulture devours the liver òf the fettered Prometheus. How could it be shown more finely and wisely that the forces streaming into us with the breathing process gnaw at the liver and that he who accomplishes in advance what is accomplished by mankind in a far future, stands there like a crucified one —how that which sinks down out of the air, eats into the liver!

Thus the initiates have expressed the mighty truths of existence in the myths. There is no myth really drawn from the Mysteries which does not express deep wisdom which can afterwards be checked. When, equipped with the knowledge of spiritual science, we approach the myths we must stand before them in reverence. They have been revealed by the higher Spiritual Beings to man so that he may first learn in pictures what he must later attain in clear concepts. More and more it will be realized that the myths contain wisdom and if one would find deepest wisdom displayed in any sphere of life, one must go to the myths. This has been known to those who have created out of the depths of art. Deep truth, for instance, underlies Richard Wagner's relation to mythology, and it has come to expression in his work in an artistic way. Our time is one which will re-ascend from a merely physical commonplaceness to a completely spiritual stream. If you look into what pulsates in our time from this standpoint you will understand in ever deeper sense the task of Spiritual Science.

Thus, starting from the study of higher worlds we have come to recognize the actual mission of Spiritual Science. It is to enable man to learn to know life, and when he is working and creating to show him what is secretly working with him when he moves his hand, when he creates with spirit, soul, and body. Through spiritual knowledge he will become more and more conscious of the beings who are his companions, and will live and create with them in harmony. Thus spiritual research will reveal to him the fullness of reality and enable him to bring knowledge and wisdom into life.

II

IN THE lecture today we shall make a rather far-reaching sweep into cosmic space. This will reveal to us, in broad outline, the inner course of world evolution, and at the same time its intimate connection with human evolution on the Earth. Everything in the universe is interconnected. To be able to follow these complicated connections naturally takes a long, long time, and it is only very gradually that man can find his way, so to speak, into the intricate workings of the cosmos.

In previous lectures you have heard how certain beings who have their abode on other cosmic bodies exercise an influence upon our own life, how they are related to what we call lymph, to the digestive fluids, also to our sense-perceptions. This will have given you a picture of the widespread operations of the spirit throughout cosmic space. We shall study a different aspect of these things today, reminding ourselves, to begin with, that our Earth, like man himself, has passed through different embodiments and will pass through others in times to come.

We look back to three previous embodiments of our Earth: to the immediately preceding embodiment which we call the Old Moon (not to be confused with our present moon); then to that of the "Sun"; and still further back to that of "Saturn." And looking forward we see prophetically that our Earth will be transformed into a "Jupiter," a "Venus" and a "Vulcan."

These are the successive embodiments of our planet Earth. If you give a little thought to these stages of our Earth's evolution, you will realize that what in occult science we call a "Sun" is—like our present sun—a heavenly body around which a number of planets revolve. When, apart from this, we also speak of a planetary Sun-existence, saying that our Earth itself in an earlier state of evolution, was "Sun," we imply, in a certain respect, that the sun which is today the centre of our planetary system, was not always a sun. It has advanced, so to speak, to the rank and dignity of a sun in the Cosmos. It was once united with the substances and forces contained in our Earth and then, taking away, as it were, what was the best and most capable of the highest development, it separated from the Earth, leaving us, together with certain forces which were destined for a slower evolution, behind. The Sun took with it certain higher beings and together with these higher beings established itself at the centre of our system. Therefore two stages earlier, what is contained in the sun today had a planetary existence only and it has risen from this to the form of existence belonging to the fixed stars. This will show you what mighty changes in evolution take place in the universe. At the outset, a sun is not a sun. A fixed star has not, from the very beginning, been a fixed star, but has had to pass through the lower school of planetary existence.

Now you may quite naturally ask me: What, then, happens when a fixed star evolves to a further stage? As truly as the Sun-existence—a fixed star existence—has risen from a planetary existence, so truly does its evolution proceed to further stages of life in the cosmos. We shall of course understand this evolution still better if we study the further evolution of our Earth.

It is true that for a certain period of its cosmic evolution our earth has been separated from the sun. The sun and its beings advance along a more rapid evolutionary path. Our earth and the beings belonging to it take a different course. But these beings, and the earth as a whole, will one day have progressed to the stage where union is again possible with the sun—after a separate existence has enabled them to complete and perfect their present phase of development. For our earth will again unite with the sun. During the stage of Earth-existence itself, the earth will reunite with the sun, just as during the same phase of evolution it separated from the sun. But during the Jupiter-stage there must again be a separation. The earth-beings must again be separated from the sun during the Jupiter-condition. Again there will be a reunion, and during the Venus-condition our earth will be united permanently with the sun, will have been taken up for all time into the sun. During the Vulcan-condition our earth will itself have become a sun within the sun and have contributed something to the sun-evolution, will have added something which, in spite of their higher rank, those beings who have always remained in the sun, could never themselves have achieved. Earth-existence was necessary in order that men might evolve as they have evolved, with a consciousness that alternates between waking and sleeping. This is connected with the separation from the sun. Beings who live always in the sun do not have day and night. The sense-consciousness which we call the clear consciousness of day and which in times to come will evolve into higher conditions, carries with it into the sun-evolution the fruits of experiences connected with the things of outer physical space. In this way the earth-

beings give something to the sun, enrich the sun. And out of
what is thus acquired on the earth, augmented by what is
acquired on the sun, the Vulcan-existence comes into being.
This Vulcan-existence is actually a higher condition than
that of our present sun-existence. The earth evolves, the
sun evolves, until they can unite to constitute the Vulcan-
existence.

You may ask me: When a planet has evolved in this way
to a sun-existence, what does this sun become in the course
of further cosmic evolution? When our earth reaches
the Venus-condition it will itself have become sun, and all
the beings on Venus are sun-beings—actually at a higher
stage than the beings of the present sun. What, then, is the
further stage of such planetary evolution?

The following will seem grotesque, even preposterous,
to those whose concepts are rooted in modern astronomy.
Nevertheless it is a truth of cosmic evolution that when a
planet like our earth has risen to sun-existence, when it has
gradually achieved union with the sun and even sun-existence is transcended, there arises, as a still higher stage of
evolution, something that in a certain sense you can perceive
in the heavens: there arises what we today call a "Zodiac"
—it is the stage higher than that of a fixed star. Thus when
beings are no longer restricted to the form of existence
belonging to a fixed star but have expanded their evolution so powerfully that it extends beyond fixed stars and
the fixed stars lie like bodies embedded in it—then a higher
stage is reached, the stage of Zodiac-existence. The forces
which work from a Zodiac upon a planetary system themselves evolved, in former ages, in a planetary system and
have advanced to the stage of a Zodiac. . ,

And now cast your minds back to the old Saturn evolution, the first embodiment of our Earth. This Saturn

once glimmered, as it were, in cosmic space, as the first herald of the dawn of our planetary existence. You know, too, that on this old Saturn the first germinal inception of our physical body was brought into being. Even at its greatest density this Saturn was not nearly as physically dense as our earth. It was a condition of utmost rarefication. That which today permeates all beings as warmth—known in occultism as "fire"—was the matter of Saturn. We may picture to ourselves that around this Saturn, this first, dawn-condition of our planetary system, there were the constellations of the Zodiac—but not yet as they are today. The single stars composing the Zodiacal constellations around that ancient Saturn were scarcely to be distinguished from each other. They glittered only very faintly, like beams of light streaming out from Saturn. The best way to picture this is to think of ancient Saturn encircled by beams of light, just as our earth is encircled by a Zodiac. And in the course of Earth-evolution itself these light-masses developed into the present star clusters comprised in the Zodiac. So that the Zodiac—to use an abstract expression—has differentiated out of that original ocean of flame. And from what did this ocean of flame itself arise?

It arose from the planetary system which preceded our own. Saturn itself was preceded by planetary evolutions in an age which, speaking in the sense of occult astronomy, can by no means be described as "time" as we understand time, for its character was rather different. But for the human mind today the concept is so fabulous that we have no word with which to express it. Speaking in analogy, however, we can say that the forces which preceded our planetary system in an earlier cycle of planetary existence went forth in the light-streams, and out of a small portion of matter gradually gathering together at the centre, this first, dawn-

23

condition of the Earth arose; this was ancient Saturn and the forces contained in the Zodiac radiated down upon it from the cosmic All.

Something rather remarkable comes to light when we compare planetary existence with zodiacal existence. The occultist makes use of two words to indicate the difference between them. He says: Everything that is contained in the Zodiac is under the sign of "Duration"; everything that is comprised within planetary existence is under the sign of "Time." You can get an idea of what this means if you remember that not even the farthest reaches of the mind can conceive of changes having taken place in the Zodiac. Each single planet may have undergone considerable change through long and greatly differing periods of evolution; the forces working in the Zodiac remain, relatively speaking, fixed and permanent. These concepts can, in any case, be only relative. The only difference in these changes of which we can conceive is in respect of the speed. Changes in the Zodiac take place slowly; changes in the planetary world and even in the existence of a fixed star take place rapidly— in comparison, that is to say, with what happens in the Zodiac.—The difference is always relative, only relative. As far as human thinking is concerned, we can say that planetary existence belongs to the sphere of the Finite, whereas Zodiacal existence belongs to the sphere of Infinitude. This, as already said, must be taken in the relative sense, but for the present it is sufficiently accurate.

And now I would ask you to pay special attention to the following: What has been achieved in a planetary existence and has become sun, ascends to "heavenly" existence, becomes zodiacal existence. And having reached zodiacal existence, what does it do? It offers itself in sacrifice! Please take account of this particular word. The first dawn-condition of the Earth, ancient Saturn, arose in a mysterious way as the result of sacrifice on the part of the Zodiac. The forces which caused the first, rarefied Saturn-masses to gather together were those which streamed down from the Zodiac, producing on Saturn the first germinal inception of physical man. This continued without cessation. You must not picture it as happening only once. Fundamentally speaking, what is happening continuously is that within what we call a planetary system the forces which evolved to a higher stage after having themselves passed through a planetary system, are sacrificed. We can say in effect: what is at first contained in a planetary system evolves to a "sun" existence, then to zodiacal existence and then has the power to be itself creative, to offer itself in sacrifice within a planetary existence. The forces from the Zodiac "rain" down continuously into the planetary existence and continuously ascend again; for that which at one time became our Zodiac must gradually ascend again. The distribution of forces in our earth existence may be conceived as follows:—on the one side forces are descending from the Zodiac and, on the other, forces are ascending to the Zodiac. Such is the mysterious interplay between the Zodiac and our earth. Forces descend and forces ascend. This is the mysterious "heavenly ladder" upon which forces are descending and ascending. These forces are indicated in various ways in the different scriptures; you find them indicated, too, in Goethe's *Faust:*

"What heavenly forces up and down are ranging,
The golden vessels interchanging."

As far as our human understanding goes, these forces began to descend during the Saturn-existence of our Earth and when the Earth-existence proper had reached its middle point, the stage had arrived when they gradually began again to ascend. We have now passed beyond the middle point of our evolution, which fell in the middle of the Atlantean epoch; and what human beings have lived through since then is a phase of existence beyond the middle point. In a certain sense, therefore, we may say that at the present time, more forces are ascending to the Zodiac than are descending from it.

When, therefore, you think of the whole Zodiac, you must picture that some of its forces are descending and some are ascending. We think of the forces which are now involved in the ascending line of evolution, collectively, as Aries, Taurus, Gemini, Cancer, Leo, Virgo, Libra—because they actually belong to these constellations. These seven constellations comprise the ascending forces. The descending forces are comprised, approximately speaking, in the five constellations of Scorpio, Sagittarius, Capricorn, Aquarius, Pisces. Thus forces rain down from the Zodiac and ascend again: seven constellations of ascending, five of descending forces. The ascending forces also correspond, in man, to the higher members of his being, to his higher, nobler attributes. The forces which are in the descending phase of evolution have first to pass through man and within him to attain to the stage at which they too can become ascending forces.

In this way you will realize that there is interaction between everything in cosmic space, that everything in cosmic space is interconnected, inter-related. But it must never be forgotten that these operations and activities are going on all the time, that they are ever-present. At any given moment in our evolution we can therefore speak of forces which are going forth from man and forces which are coming in; forces are descending and forces are ascending. For all and each of these forces there comes, at some point, the moment when from being descending forces they are transformed into ascending forces. All forces which eventually become ascending forces are at first descending forces. They descend, so to say, as far as man. In man they acquire the power to ascend.

At the middle point of its evolution, when our Earth had passed through the three planetary stages of Saturn, Sun, Moon, had reached the fourth planetary condition, having in front of it the stages of Jupiter, Venus and Vulcan (as Earth, therefore, it is midway in the span of its existence) —it had passed through three "life-conditions" (also called "rounds"). It has passed through three of these life-conditions and is now in the fourth; it has passed through three "form-conditions"—the arupic, the rupic, and the astral, leading down to physical existence. Therefore in respect of the "form-conditions," our Earth is in the middle phase of its evolution. As physical Earth, in the fourth form-condition of the fourth life-condition of the fourth planetary existence it has had upon it three great races: the first, the Polarian race; the second, the Hyperborean race; the third, the Lemurian race. The Atlantean race is the fourth. In the Atlantean race, humanity was in the middle of those phases of evolution of which we are speaking. Since the middle of the Atlantean epoch humanity has passed beyond this middle point. And since the middle of the Atlantean epoch there have begun, for men in general, those conditions in which the ascending forces preponderate. If we were speaking of the proportion of forces descending from and ascending to the Zodiac before the middle of the Atlantean epoch, we should have to say: they were in equal proportion. We should have to speak differently of the conditions then prevailing, enumerating as the ascending forces: Aries, Taurus, Gemini, Cancer, Leo, Virgo—counting Libra with the other descending forces.

But something else is connected with all this. You must realize that in speaking of these cosmic processes, we are not speaking of physical or etheric bodies but of beings indwelling the several heavenly bodies. When we speak of man in terms of Spiritual Science we say that the whole man—and we think of man only in this sense—is a sevenfold being, consisting of physical body, etheric body, astral body, ego, spirit-self, life-spirit, spirit-man. His development is not yet complete but will be when his sevenfold being has fully developed. But in the great cosmic All there are beings other than man, beings of a different nature. There are, for example, beings in the cosmos of whom we cannot say that, like man, they have the physical body as one of their members. There are beings of whom we must speak differently. The members of which man is composed can be enumerated as follows:

7. Spirit-Man
6. Life-Spirit
5. Spirit-Self
4. Ego
3. Astral Body
2. Etheric Body
1. Physical Body

Now there are beings whose lowest member is the etheric body; they too are sevenfold, having an eighth member, higher than spirit-man. We begin to enumerate thus: etheric body, astral body, and so forth, finishing with a member above our spirit-man (Atma). There are other beings whose lowest member is the astral body; above spirit-man they have an eighth and yet a ninth member. Again there are beings whose lowest member is the 'I,' the ego, and who therefore have not a physical nor an etheric nor an astral body in our sense but whose Ego streams outwards without the three sheaths. They are therefore beings who send forth 'Egos' in all directions. These Beings have an eighth, a ninth, and a tenth member; they are described in the Apocalypse as beings who are "full of eyes". Then there are beings in whom spirit-self (Manas) is the lowest member. They have yet an eleventh member. And finally there are beings whose lowest member is the life-spirit and who have yet a twelfth member. You must therefore think of beings who, just as man's lowest member is a physical body, have life-spirit (Budhi) as their lowest member and above, a highest member best designated by the number 12. These are most sublime beings, far transcending everything that man is able to conceive. How is it possible to form any kind of idea of these most wonderful, most sublime beings?

When we try to characterize man, in one aspect, it is obvious that with respect to the universe, he is a being who *receives*. The things and beings of the world are outspread around you; you perceive them, you form concepts of them. Just imagine that the world around you were empty, or dark. You could have no perceptions, nor would there be anything of which you could form concepts. You have to rely upon receiving from outside the content of your inner world. It is characteristic of man that he is a being who *receives*; he receives the content of his soul-life, his inner life, from outside; things must exist in the world if his soul is to have content. The nature of man's etheric body is such that it could experience nothing in itself were it not beholden to the whole surrounding universe for all experiences, for everything that enters into it. These beings of whom I have just told you, who have life-spirit as their lowest member, are in an entirely different position. In respect of their life, these beings are not dependent upon receiving anything from outside; they are "givers," they are themselves creative. You know from what I have often told you, that the 'I,' the ego, works in the etheric body and that 'Budhi' is nothing else than a transformed etheric body. In respect of substance, therefore, the life-spirit too is an ether body. The twelfth member of these sublime beings is also an 'ether body' but one which pours forth life, which works in the world in such a way that it does not receive life but gives it forth, offers life in perpetual sacrifice.

And now let us ask: Can we conceive of a being who is in any way connected with us and who radiates life into our universe? Is it possible to conceive of life that is perpetually streaming into the world, imbuing the world with life?

Let us think for a moment of what was said at the beginning of the lecture, namely that there are ascending and descending forces—forces that are ascending to the Zodiac and forces that are descending from the Zodiac. How has man reached a position which makes it possible for something to stream from within him? What has happened to man that enables something to stream forth from him? He has reached this position because his ego, after long, long preparation, has steadily unfolded and developed. This I, this ego, has been in course of preparation for long, long ages. For truth to tell, the object of all existence in the Saturn-condition, the Sun-condition and the Moon-condition—when the sheaths into which the I was to be received were produced—was to prepare for the I. In those earlier conditions, other beings created the dwelling-place for the I. Now, on the earth, the dwelling-place was at the stage where the I could take root in man and from then onwards the I began to work upon the outer, bodily sheaths from within.

The fact that the ego is able to work from within has also brought about a surplus, a surplus of ascending forces; there was no longer a state of parity. Before the ego was able to work within man, the ascending forces gradually evolved until the middle point had been reached; and when the ego actually entered into man the ascending and the descending forces had reached the stage where they were in 'balance.' At the entry of the ego, the ascending and the descending forces were in balance and it rests with man to turn the scales in the right direction. That is why the occultists have called the constellation which was entered at the time when the ego itself began to operate, the 'Balance' (Libra). Up to the end of Virgo, preparation was being made for the deeds of the ego in our planetary evolution, but the ego had not itself begun to work. When Libra had been reached the ego itself began to participate and this was a most important moment in its evolution.

Just think what it means that the ego had reached this stage of evolution:

From then on it was possible for the ego to participate in the work of the forces belonging to the Zodiac, to reach into the Zodiac. The more the ego strives for the highest point of its evolution, the more it works into the Zodiac. There is nothing that happens in the innermost core of the ego that has not its consequences right up to the very Zodiac. And inasmuch as man with his ego lays the foundations for his development to Atma, or spirit-man, he develops, stage by stage, the forces which enable him to work upwards into the sphere of Libra, the Balance, in the Zodiac. He will attain full power over Libra in the Zodiac when his ego has developed to Atma, or spirit-man. He will then be a being from whom something streams out, who has passed

31

out of the sphere of Time into the sphere of Duration, of Eternity.

Such is the path of man. But there are other beings whose *lowest* sphere of operation is man's *highest*. Let us try to conceive of these beings whose lowest sphere of operation is man's highest (Libra in the Zodiac). When we relate man to the Zodiac, he reaches to Libra. The Being whose innermost nature belongs wholly to the Zodiac, whose forces belong wholly to the Zodiac, who only manifests in planetary life through his lowest member, which corresponds to Libra (as man's lowest member corresponds to Pisces)— this is the Being who spreads life throughout the whole of our universe:

	Aries ..... 12th member	
	Taurus .... 11th member	
	Gemini .... 10th member	
	Cancer ..... 9th member	"Mystical Lamb"
	Leo .... 8th member	
7th Spirit-Man	Virgo ...... 7th member	
6th Life-Spirit	Libra ...... 6th member	
5th Spirit-Self	Scorpio	
4th Ego	Sagittarius	
3rd Astral Body	Capricorn	
2nd Etheric Body	Aquarius	
1st Physical Body ...	Pisces	

Just as man receives life into himself, so does this Being radiate life through the whole of our universe. This is the Being Who has the power to make the great sacrifice and Who is inscribed in the Zodiac as the Being Who for the sake of our world offers Himself in sacrifice. Just as man strives upwards into the Zodiac, so does this Being send us His sacrificial gift from Aries—which is related to Him as Libra is related to man. And just as man turns his ego upwards to Libra, so does this Being radiate His very Self over our sphere in sacrifice. This Being is called the "Mystical Lamb," for Lamb and Aries are the same; therefore the description 'Sacrificial Lamb' or 'Ram' is given to Christ. Christ belongs to the cosmos as a whole. His I, his Ego, reaches to Aries and thus He becomes Himself the "Great Sacrifice," is related with the whole of mankind and in a certain sense the beings and forces present on the earth are His creations. The configuration of forces is such that He could become the Creator of these beings in the constellation of Aries, or the Lamb. The designation "Sacrificial Lamb" or "Mystical Lamb" is drawn from the heavens themselves.

This is one of the aspects revealed to us when from our circumscribed existence we look up into the heavens and perceive the interworking of heavenly forces and beings in cosmic space. Gradually we begin to realize that the forces streaming from heavenly body to heavenly body are akin to those forces which stream from one human soul to another as love and hate. We perceive soul-forces streaming from star to star and learn to recognize the heavenly script which records for us what is wrought and effected by those forces in cosmic space.

III

THE purpose of these lectures is to bring still loftier concepts to those more advanced students of theosophy who have been familiar for some time with its world-conception and—which is much more important—have become at home in its way of thinking and feeling. This will make it more difficult for the later-comers to follow; perhaps they are well able to follow with their understanding, but it will become increasingly difficult for them to regard as sound and reasonable what is brought forward from the higher sections of theosophy. Much goodwill, therefore, will be required of new-comers to follow these group-lectures with the understanding of feeling and perception. Yet we should make no progress if we had no opportunity of throwing light upon the higher realms of spiritual existence as well. That then is the purpose of these lectures.

Now in the last lecture I gave you a picture of the evolution of our whole planetary system. Before that we had considered the planetary system itself in so far as the various planets are peopled by beings who have an influence on our human body. What is to be brought forward today will link on to these two previous studies. We will extend still further our picture of the planetary system and learn some of the mysteries of our cosmic existence from a spiritual aspect.

In the numerous popular accounts of the origin of our planetary system one is first led back to a kind of original mist, to a vast fog-like structure, a nebula, out of which our sun and its planets have somehow agglomerated, although for the driving force in this process only physical forces, as a rule, are taken into account. This is called the "Kant-La- -place theory," though it is somewhat modified today, and those who have arrived at an intellectual grasp of the gradual agglomeration of the different planets out of the original nebula up to the condition in which they and our earth now exist, are very proud of their intelligence. They continually emphasize that it is but little in keeping with the present important advance in science to speak of spiritual forces and spiritual beings in this separation of the heavenly bodies out of the nebula. Various popular books, too, describe such statements as completely backward and superstitious.

Now the intelligence of a student of theosophy would suffice for an understanding of what is brought forward in this way. But he goes somewhat further. It is clear to him that the physical forces of attraction and repulsion were not enough. It is clear that all sorts of other things played a part. Theosophy has still to put up with being proclaimed thoroughly dense and stupid and a dreadful superstition by popular official science—which one could perhaps call "antisophy." But we are living in an age which in a remarkable way is full of hope for the theosophist. It could be said that the theories, opinions and knowledge that modern popular science forms from its own facts look like tiny, gasping, dwarf-like creatures which run puffing and blowing at a considerable distance behind the facts. The facts of modern science are actually far, far ahead of the "belief" of modern science—only that is not recognized. I should only like to

35

remind you of how we have often spoken here of the activity of the astral body during the night, of how the astral body at night works at upbuilding the physical and etheric bodies and ridding them of the fatigue substances they have acquired during the day. To express the sentence in this form would simply strike modern science as something not fit for polite society. But facts speak a plain language. When, for example, we can read in an American paper today that a researcher has established the theory that the sleep activity in man is an involving, constructive one, whereas on the other hand the waking activity is a destructive one, you have again a proof of how modern science runs after the facts like little dwarfs who cannot keep up. In the world-conception of theosophy you have the great illuminating views that are drawn out of a spiritual conception of the world.

When we consider the origin of our present solar system theosophically we need in no wise—nor in other fields—directly contradict what is put forward by physical science. For theosophy has no objections to make in respect of what physical science strives to know—that is, what eyes could have seen in the successive phases of evolution. If at the time of the original nebula someone had placed a chair out in universal space, had sat on it for a sufficiently long lifetime and had watched how the different globes had gathered themselves into balls and separated off, with physical eyes he would have seen nothing but what physical science has affirmed. But that would be just the same as if two observers reported that a man gave another a box on the ear and one of them should say: The man was furiously angry with the other and that made him shoot out his hand and give the other a box on the ear. The second observer might say: I saw nothing of anger or passion, I only saw the hand move and inflict the blow.—That is the external, materialistic description, the method employed by modern science; it does not contradict the spiritual examination of the facts. However, the man who believes that this materialistic description is the only one naturally feels that his scientific eminence is vastly superior to everything put forward by spiritual research. The modified Kant-Laplace theory may definitely hold good as an external event, but within the whole forming of globes, within this whole crystallizing of the separate cosmic globes, spiritual forces and spiritual beings were at work.

The experimenter shows us today in a beautiful way how this Kant-Laplace theory can proceed. One need only take a fairly small ball of oil that swims in water. Then one can very easily put a little cardboard disk in the plane of the equator through this ball and put a needle through the centre. Now one rotates the needle very rapidly, little oil-balls split off, and it is easy to picture a cosmic system in miniature and to show how a cosmic system has separated itself off into globes in space. The experimenter has only forgotten one thing. He forgets that he himself was there, that he made the necessary preparation, that he then rotated the needle and that what cannot go of itself on a miniature scale cannot go of itself in the universe. Out there it is supposed to go of itself. Things are not in the least so very difficult to comprehend, but the right physical principles are so worn out that those who do not want to see them really need not see them. So, spiritual forces and spiritual beings were active in this whole process of planet formation and we will now learn something about it.

I must remind you of the often-repeated fact that before our Earth became "Earth" it had gone through earlier embodiments, other planetary conditions—the Saturn, Sun, and Moon conditions, and only then advanced to its present

Earth condition. Now picture vividly ancient Saturn, floating in space in the far-distant past, the first embodiment of our Earth. Within the whole being of Saturn there was as yet nothing at all of what we see round us today as our plants, minerals, animals. Saturn consisted in the beginning of nothing but the very first rudiments of humanity. We speak of ancient Saturn as of nothing but a sort of conglomeration of human beings. Man existed at that time only in the first rudiments of his physical body. Ancient Saturn was simply composed of individual physical human bodies—somewhat as a mulberry or blackberry is composed of nothing but single tiny berries. It was surrounded by an atmosphere, as today our Earth is surrounded by air, but in relation to what we know as atmosphere today it was spiritual. It was entirely of a spiritual nature and within the Saturn evolution man began his first development. Then came a time when Saturn went through a state similar to man's condition between death and rebirth in Devachan. One calls this state of a cosmic body, Pralaya. Thus Saturn went through a sort of devachanic state and when it entered again upon a kind of externally perceptible existence, it emerged as our Earth's second planetary stage, as Sun. This Sun-condition brought the human being again further. Certain beings which had remained behind now emerged at the side of the human kingdom, so that there were then two kingdoms on the Sun. Then came a Pralaya, a devachanic condition, after which the whole planet was transformed into the Moon-condition; and so it continued, again a Pralaya, until the Moon passed over into our Earth.

When our Earth came forth from the purely spiritual devachanic state and received for the first time a kind of externally perceptible existence, it was not like it is today. In fact, seen externally, it could really be pictured as a kind of great primordial nebula, as our physical science describes. Only we must think of this primordial mist as immense, far greater than the present earth, extending far beyond the outermost planets now belonging to our solar system— far beyond Uranus. To spiritual science what is seen coming forth from a spiritual condition is not merely a kind of physical mist. To describe it as a kind of mist and nothing more is about as sensible as if a man who has seen another should reply to a question as to what he saw: I saw muscles which are attached to bones and blood—simply describing the physical aspect. For in the primordial mist there were a multitude of spiritual forces and spiritual beings. They belonged to it, and what happened in this primordial mist was a consequence of the deeds of spiritual beings. All that the physicist sees when he sets out a chair in cosmic space and watches the proceedings, he describes just as the observer who denied the passion and anger and described only the moving hand. In reality, what took place there—the separating off of cosmic bodies and globes—was the act of spiritual beings; in the primordial mist, therefore, we must see the garment, the outer manifestation, of a multitude of spiritual beings.

They are spiritual beings at very varied stages of evolution. They do not arise out of a nothingness, they have a past behind them. They have the Saturn, Sun, Moon-past behind them. They have gone through all this and now they stand before the task of turning into deeds all that they have gone through. They have to "do" what they have learnt on Saturn, Sun, Moon, and they stand at most diverse heights of development. Among them are beings who were as advanced on ancient Saturn as man is on Earth today. These have already passed through their human stage on Saturn and thus stand far above man at the outset of the Earth's evolution. Other beings are there who went through their human stage on the Sun, others who did so on the Moon. The human being waited to go through his human stage on the Earth. Even if we consider only this fourfold hierarchy we have a series of different beings at different stages of evolution.

We call the beings who went through their human stage on the Sun, the "Fire-Spirits," but you must not imagine that they were externally like the men of today. They went through their human stage in a different external form. The ancient Sun planet had an extraordinarily fine light substance, far lighter than our present substance. At that time there was no kind of solid or fluid, nothing but the gaseous element existed, and the bodies of the Fire-Spirits in spite of their being of human rank were gaseous bodies. One can go through the human stage in cosmic evolution in the most varied forms. Only the Earth-man goes through it in the flesh on Earth. The beings who had human rank on the Moon and who were already at a higher stage than man went through it in a kind of watery condition.

Thus these spirits and a whole host of others were united with the primordial mist that lay at the starting-point of our Solar system. Thus, for instance, you can readily understand that what began for man upon Saturn began in some way for other beings upon the Sun. As on Saturn the first rudiments of the physical body began, so on the Sun other beings followed, just as in schools different primary pupils are always following on. These beings have only advanced to the point of being physically incorporated in our contemporary animals. On the Moon followed beings who are present in our contemporary plants, and our present minerals have only been added on the Earth. These are our youngest companions in evolution whose pains and joys I described to you in a previous lecture. Thus in the original mist there were not only advanced beings but those too who had not yet reached the human stage.

We must now add to those which I have enumerated, beings I have spoken of as lagging behind at certain stages of cosmic evolution. Let us take the Fire-Spirits. They had already attained their human stage on the Sun, and now, on the Earth, they are highly exalted beings, two stages above man. They are so advanced that not until man has ascended through the Jupiter and Venus existence to the Vulcan existence will he be mature for such an existence as that of the lofty Sun-Spirits at the beginning of the Earth's development. But now there were beings who had remained behind, who should have progressed on the Sun as far as the Fire-Spirits, but who for certain reasons stayed behind. They could not develop to the full height which the Fire-Spirits had reached when the Earth stood at the outset of its evolution.

You will all remember that at the very beginning of its evolution the Earth was still one body with sun and moon—and this you can easily combine with the theory of the original mist or nebula. If you were, therefore, to stir together the three heavenly bodies, earth, sun, moon, in a gigantic cosmic cauldron you would get a body which at one time existed. Then came the time when the sun drew out and left earth and moon, to be followed by a time when the moon too drew out and left our earth as it is today with the sun on one side and the moon on the other. We now ask ourselves how it came about that three bodies arose out of the one. You will easily see why that happened when you remember that highly-evolved beings, standing two stages above man, were present in the primordial mist—unified with its external existence. They would have had nothing directly to do on such a cosmic body as our present-day earth, they needed a dwelling place with quite different characteristics. On the other hand the human being would have been consumed in an existence united with the sun. He needed a weakened, milder existence. It was essential then that through the action of the Fire-Spirits the sun should be withdrawn from the earth and made into their scene of action. It was not a merely physical event: we must understand it as the deed of the Fire-Spirits themselves. They drew out their dwelling place and all they needed as substances from the earth and made their theatre the sun. By virtue of their nature they can endure that immense velocity of development. If the human being were exposed to such a velocity, then scarcely were he young when he would at once become old. All evolution went on at a furious tempo. Only such beings as stood two stages higher than man could bear the sun-existence. They drew away together with the sun and left behind the earth with the moon.

Now we can answer the question too why the moon had to separate from the earth. If the moon had remained united with the earth then man could again not have sustained his existence. The moon had to be thrust out, for it would have mummified man's whole development. Men would not have undergone such a rapid development as they would had the sun remained, but they would have been carbonized, dried to mummies; their evolution would have been such a slow one that they would have become mummified. In order to produce just the degree of development useful to man, the moon with its forces and its subordinate beings had to be thrust out. And so likewise united with the moon are those beings which I have described as remaining at a time of life comparable to that reached today on earth by a seven-year-old child. As they only go through an existence such as a human existence up to the age of seven, when only the physical body is developed, they need a dwelling-place such as the moon. When you add the fact that not only these various beings were united with the original nebula, but a whole series more, standing at very varied stages of evolution, then you will understand that not only these cosmic bodies, earth, sun, moon, separated from the nebula, but other cosmic bodies too. Indeed they all agglomerated as separate globes because scenes of action had to be found for the varying stages of evolution of the different beings.

Thus there were beings at the very beginning of our Earth who were scarcely fitted to take part in further development, who were still so young in their whole evolution that any further step would have destroyed them. They had to receive a sphere of action, so to speak, on which they could preserve their complete youthfulness. All other fields of action existed to give dwelling-places to those who were already more advanced. For the beings who arose last of all during the Moon existence, and who therefore had stayed behind at a very early evolutionary stage, a field of action had to be separated out. This scene of action was the cosmic body which we call "Uranus," and which therefore has but slight connection with our earthly existence. Uranus has become the theatre for beings which had to remain at a very backward stage.

Then evolution proceeded. Apart from Uranus, all that forms our universe was contained in an original pap-like mass. Greek mythology calls this condition "Chaos." Then Uranus separated out, the rest remaining still in the Chaos. Within it were beings who in their development stood precisely at the stage at which we human beings stood when our Earth passed through the Saturn condition. And for these beings a special theatre, "Saturn," was created, since standing at that stage, only just beginning their existence,

43

they could not share in all that came later. Thus a second cosmic body split off, Saturn, which you still see in the heavens today. It arose through the fact that there were beings who stood at the same stage as man at the Saturn-time of the Earth. Whereas Saturn arose as a separate cosmic body, everything else that belongs to our present planetary system, the earth with all its beings, was still in this original pap-like mass. Only Uranus and Saturn were outside.

The next thing that took place was the separating of another planet which had to become the scene for a certain stage of development. That was the planet Jupiter, the third to split off from the misty mass which for us is actually the earth. At the time of Jupiter's separation, sun, moon, as well as all the other planets of our system, were still united with the earth. When Jupiter had split off there gradually arose the forerunners of contemporary humanity. That is to say, our present human beings emerged again just as a new plant comes out of the seed. The human seeds had gradually formed during the conditions of ancient Saturn, Sun and Moon, and now while the sun was still linked with the earth these human seeds came out again.

But now the human beings would not have been able to evolve further, they could not support the tempo as long as the sun remained with the earth. Then something came about which we can well understand when we are clear that the beings we have called the Fire-Spirits took their scene of action away from the earth. The sun pressed out and we have now sun, with earth and moon together. During this time Mars—in a way which would take too much time to relate now in detail—had again formed a theatre for particular beings, and in its further advance Mars actually passed through the earth and moon and left behind what today we know as iron. Hence Mars was the cause of the iron particles deposited in living beings, that is, in the blood. Now someone could say: That is not so very remarkable, iron is everywhere. For just as other bodies were in the primordial mist, so too was Mars with the iron which it left behind. Iron is in all the other planets as well!—Science today, however, wonderfully confirms what is given here from the teaching of spiritual science. You will remember that I once showed you how one passes symbolically from the green sap of the plant, chlorophyll, to the blood of man. Plants arose at the period before this passage of Mars had taken place and have preserved their characteristic. Then the iron was deposited in the beings more highly organized than the plants, permeating the red blood. Thus what has recently been found in a Zurich laboratory is in complete accordance with these spiritual-scientific facts, namely, that blood cannot be compared with chlorophyll, simply because it was deposited later. We must not imagine that blood depends in any way on the substantiality of the chemical element "iron." I say that especially, because someone might say that one can speak of no connection at all of chlorophyll with the blood. Today science makes the discovery that the blood is to be traced back to the element "iron"—whereas chlorophyll contains no iron. It is nevertheless in the fullest harmony with what Spiritual Science has to say, it is only a matter of looking at things in the right light.

Then for reasons which we have already stated, the moon separated and we have the earth by itself and the present moon as its satellite. To the sun withdrew all the beings of an essentially higher order than man, whom we have called the Fire-Spirits. But there were certain beings which had not ascended high enough to be able really to endure the sun existence. You must be clear that they were beings exalted far above man, but still not so far advanced as to be able, like the Fire-Spirits, to live on the sun. Dwelling-places had to be created for them. None of the other theatres could have served them, for those were for beings of another nature, who had by no means attained the great age of the beings who, though belonging to the Fire-Spirits, had not quite kept up with them in cosmic evolution. In the main there were two species of beings who had remained behind, and two special arenas were therefore formed for them through the severing of Mercury and Venus from the sun. Mercury and Venus are two planets which have split off as the centres for those Fire-Spirits 'who are exalted far above human existence, yet who could not have supported the sun-existence. So you have Mercury in the neighbourhood of the sun as arena for those beings who had not been able to live with the Fire-Spirits on the sun, and Venus as arena for beings who in a certain respect had remained behind the Mercury beings but who yet stood far above man.

Thus you have seen these various cosmic bodies originate out of the primoridal mist from inner causes, from spiritually-inspired activities. If one keeps to the physical alone, matters take their course in the way depicted by modern science, but the point is to learn to know the spiritual causes by which things have become what they are. Inside the primordial mist, the beings have themselves created the dwelling-places in which they could live. Now these various beings who were, so to say, harmoniously side by side before they had separated, did not remain without connection. On the contrary, they work through one another throughout. The influence of the Mercury and Venus beings on the earth is of a quite special interest. Put yourselves back into the time when the sun and then the moon released itself from the earth and man began his existence in his present form. He has acquired this existence in the present form through the fact that one of the Sun-Spirits forbore—if I may so express it—from continuing his existence on the sun, but united himself with the moon. In this way a lofty regent of the moon arose. Beings of a lower order existed on the moon, but one of the Sun-Spirits united himself with the moon-existence. This Sun-Spirit who is therefore really a displaced Sun-Spirit in the universe is, as divine, spiritual being, Yahve, Jehovah, the regent of the moon. We shall see why that came about if we consider the following.

We have seen that if the sun had remained united to the earth man would have been consumed by the swift course of development, and if the moon and its forces alone had worked upon man he would have been mummified. Precisely through the harmony of sun and moon forces arose the equilibrium that keeps man in the present tempo of evolution. When the Earth had come over from the old Moon, man had his physical body from Saturn, his etheric body from the Sun and his astral body from the Moon. But because he had the three bodies and the seed with the three bodies now began to develop, he had a very different form. You would open your eyes in amazement if I should describe it to you, for the present human form has arisen quite slowly and gradually from the time of the moon-separation. But the base, inferior moon-forces could not have given man his present form. They could certainly have given him a form, but an inferior one. If the moon-forces had remained with the earth they would have *held him fast* in one form. Forces that *give* the form must proceed from the moon, while forces that continually *alter* the form proceed from the sun. But in order that the present human form should arise, a molder, a modeler of form, must work from the moon; it was not possible otherwise. At that time therefore began the development of the ego-man. The fourth member of the human entity arose and Yahve gave the human being the nucleus to a form which would enable him to become an ego-bearer.

Now man was not yet capable of carrying out the work of which I have told you. I have explained that man's ego works upon his astral, etheric, and physical bodies. But he can only begin this work gradually. As a child needs teachers, so when man was already prepared to become an ego-bearer, he needed a stimulus on earth to enable him to advance, and there were two "stimulators." You can think whence, from the whole cosmic evolution, they came.

The beings who stood nearest to man were the Venus and Mercury beings. Until, at the end of the Atlantean Age, man could make the first feeble efforts to work independently with his ego upon the three bodies—for that was just possible at the end of the Atlantean Age—he had to have teachers. These teachers were beings of Venus and Mercury, and they went on working far beyond the Age of Atlantis. But they are not to be looked on as we look on our present teachers; the Venus beings must rather be thought of as those who endowed man with his intellectuality. Men knew nothing at all of this; just as the different human fluids work upon man, so did the forces of these beings influence him until he could work upon his bodies independently. What we find in man today as intelligence was mediated to him through the spirits who remained behind on Venus as Fire-Spirits of a lesser order. In addition to these were other teachers and they were in fact perceived consciously as teachers by men who attained clairvoyance—the teachers of the great Mysteries of ancient times. In the far past there was not only that all-embracing influence of the Venus-Spirits who worked more or less on mankind as a whole, there were also Mystery centres where the most advanced human beings received instruction spiritually from the Fire-Spirits. The exalted Fire-Spirits of Mercury instructed in the Mysteries; there they appeared—if we may say so—in a spiritual embodiment and were the teachers of the first initiates. Just as the first initiates became the teachers of the great masses of mankind, so did the beings of Mercury work as the teachers of the first initiates. From this you may realize that the beings of other stars have an influence upon man, but the very complicated nature of this influence can be seen from the following.

You remember that in my *Theosophy** we roughly divide the human being by saying that he consists of physical body, etheric body, astral body, ego, spirit-self, life-spirit, spirit-man. The more correct division, as you know, is physical, etheric, astral bodies, then the three soul-forces in which the ego emerges—sentient soul, intellectual or mind soul, consciousness soul—and that only then we have spirit-self or Manas, life-spirit or Budhi, spirit-man or Atma. Thus the soul-element is inserted as sentient soul, intellectual soul, consciousness soul. If we follow man's evolution on the Earth we can say that to the three constituents brought over from the Moon, the first development to be added was the sentient soul, then arose the intellectual soul, and not till towards the end of Atlantean times, when man learnt for the first time to say "I" to himself, did the consciousness-soul arise. Since then man can begin to work consciously from within upon the members of his being. If we divide man thus into body, soul, spirit, then we have to divide the soul again into sentient soul, intellectual soul, consciousness soul. These evolved gradually, and the consciousness soul could as yet have no influence, for it arose only as the last. These members had therefore to be kindled from without, and be-

* Rudolf Steiner, *Theosophy*. Anthroposophic Press, Inc, New York.

49

ings from outside were active. Mars in fact worked on the sentient soul, the already-separated Mercury with its beings worked on the origin of the intellectual soul, and Jupiter, which had been in existence the longest, worked on the origin of the consciousness soul.

Thus in the soul-nature of man we have the working of the three cosmic bodies, of Mars in the sentient soul, Mercury in the intellectual soul, Jupiter in the consciousness soul, and inasmuch as spirit-self presses into the consciousness soul, Venus with its beings is active. Mercury was also active with regard to the first initiates, so that the Mercury beings exercised a twofold activity, the one quite unconscious to man inasmuch as they developed his intellectual soul, and then as well they were the first teachers of the initiates when they worked in a fully-conscious way. The Mercury beings had thus a continuous double activity, rather as many country schoolmasters instruct the children and cultivate the land allotted to them. The Mercury beings had to develop the intellectual soul and besides that had to be the great schoolmasters of the great initiates. All these things can also be grasped by pure logic.

Now you can perhaps ask why should just Jupiter work on the consciousness soul, since it is such a distant planet. But these things are not investigated on logical grounds, but by investigating the facts of the spiritual worlds. There you would perceive it as a fact that the consciousness soul is kindled by Jupiter beings, to whose help come, on the other hand, laggard Venus beings. Things cannot be fitted into an external scheme in the activity of the cosmos; one must realize that when a planet has already fulfilled a task, its beings can later fulfill another task as well. In the course of the second race of humanity Jupiter beings co-operated on the perfecting of the etheric body; then they themselves advanced a stage, and when the human being was far enough on for his consciousness soul to develop, they had to intervene again and help in its development. What is working in space enters into joint activity in most varied ways; one cannot pass from one activity to another in any sort of schematic way.

So you see how the physicist when he looks out into the universe sees only the external bodies of spiritual organisms, and how spiritual science leads us to the spiritual foundations which bring about what the physicist sees. We have not been giving ourselves up to the illusion of the man who takes the little ball of oil and forgets that he himself turns it. We have sought for the beings who themselves drew out the globes of the planets which we perceive. We have not fallen into the illusion of thinking that if we are not there, the whole thing does not go on revolving. We have sought the "revolver," the one who stands behind as the actual spiritually active being—so that one can always find full accord between what is said by Spiritual Science and discovered by official science. Only you can never derive what Spiritual Science says from the facts of science. You would then at most come to an analogy. If on the other hand the spiritual facts have been found by occult means, then, if you disregard what official science has yet to find, they will every time be in accord with what the physicist too has to say. So the theosophist can support the physicist. He knows very well that an occurrence in the physical realm may be just what the physicist describes, but in addition there is always the spiritual process. This does not prevent many scientists from feeling very superior and considering the theosophist a poor simpleton, or something worse. But the theosophist can look on quite calmly. It will be quite different in fifty years' time, for the continuation of merely materialistic science would do great harm to the health and well-being of mankind if things were to remain as they are today, and if spiritual science were not to combat them.

IV

ToDAY we shall deal with a subject that is connected with the vast far-reaching view into cosmic space that we entered upon in our last lecture. We shall go more closely into the spiritual evolution that lies within spatial and material evolution than we did before. In the last lecture we saw how spiritual beings guide those mighty evolutionary processes which ordinary physical science describes to us inaccurately, but Theosophy or spiritual science exactly and accurately.

We have seen how the separate planets, the separate bodies of our cosmic system, arise from a common original substance, and have recognized that spiritual beings of various kinds are active in all this evolution. We have pointed out too in former lectures how spiritual science does not see merely physical material objects in the bodies of our cosmic system, but linked with the physical and material, spiritual beings of various grades. These may be beings of the most exalted order who raise evolution, thus benefiting the whole system, or they may be spiritual beings of a lower kind who hinder and destroy. Yet we must be clear that what seems to be hindrance and destruction is in the long run again membered into the wisdom of the whole system. One might therefore say: When something apparently destructive, retarding and evil exists anywhere, then evolution in its whole course will be so wisely guided that even this evil, this de-

53

struction and hindrance will be reversed and changed into the good. Today however we want to bring about a living feeling of the existence of such spiritual beings as belong to the "creative beings"—considering first those of an exalted order. Man must work in evolution for a long time yet, before he ascends to the rank of a "creative" being. We will consider in particular those beings who participated in the structure of our cosmic system when the Earth began its evolution in our universe as Saturn.

The Earth began its evolution as Saturn and advanced through the Sun and Moon evolutions up to its present formation. Everything on that Saturn cosmic body was, however, quite different from the nature of our present earthly planet. On Saturn there were no solid rocky masses, what we call the mineral world in the modern sense, nor was there water in the modern sense, not even air; what was present at that time could only be compared with warmth among our elements today, with "fire," as one says in occultism. You would certainly not get a right idea if you thought that this Saturn fire looked like the modern flame of gas or candle. To have the right conception you must call to mind what pulses up and down in your own body—you must recollect the fundamental difference existing between a lower creature of the animal world, which has preserved certain stages of evolution, and the human being. A lower creature has the warmth of its surroundings. An amphibian has no inner warmth of its own; it has the warmth of its surroundings. It is as cold or as warm as its surroundings. Man has his own internal, equable warmth, as indeed he must have. His organism must ensure that when it is cold outside, he can nevertheless maintain his warmth at a certain temperature, and you know that when disturbances such as fever etc. enter this warmth, the health of the whole body is disturbed as well. The point is that man has an inner degree of warmth and he must think of some underlying force that creates it. This force is not water, not the solid, not air, it is an element for itself, and this element alone was present on ancient Saturn, the first embodiment of our Earth. If you had gone for a walk at that time in universal space—naturally that is a phantasy but it helps to form an idea of the condition—you would not have seen Saturn, for in the earliest stage it sent out no light at all. To shed light the cosmic body must first become a sun, or be united with a sun and so become luminous. If you approached ancient Saturn you would have noticed in its neighborhood that there was warmth, you would think that there was a space filled with warmth, you would enter a space like an oven. The existence of ancient Saturn would have been realized through this force of warmth alone. It was a rarefied material substance of which modern man can scarcely form a right idea —least of all a learned physicist—but it was present, a condition finer than gas, finer than air, and all that existed of man at that time, namely, the first rudiments of the physical body, consisted of this substance. If you could eliminate today everything except the warmth of your blood then you would have an idea of those first rudiments of the human being. That, however, could not be done, since one cannot live like that. Today with our mineral kingdom, fluid kingdom, etc., we cannot live as the human being lived on ancient Saturn. At that time one could do so. But today you must think away all that you have of juices, tissues, solid parts, even the air that you take in as oxygen. You must conceive solely and alone that which remains over—naturally in quite a different form—namely, the warmth contained in your blood: a physical body consisting only of

55

warmth! It is a horrible idea for a modern natural scientist —but therefore one that is all the more correct and real.

Such was the rudimentary germ of man—his physical body. All the other beings which are on the earth today— animals—plants—minerals—were not in existence on Saturn. Saturn at that time consisted solely of human germs which were clustered together like the tiny berries which form a blackberry. In this way the Saturn-globe was a great berry made up purely of tiny berries which were the human beings. If we were to examine the surroundings of Saturn somewhat as we test our earth's surroundings and find a mantle of air in which are structures of mist, clouds etc., we should find nothing of a material nature. We should find in the Saturn mantle spiritual substance, spiritual beings, and these were at a much higher level than man in his first rudiments.

We will now occupy ourselves with a definite order of beings who were linked with the Saturn existence. There we find the Spirits of Will, then the Spirits of Wisdom, Spirits of Movement, of Form, of Personality, and so forth. To- day we will turn our attention especially to the Spirits of Form for the reason that they have played an important role in the beginning of our evolution. From the whole ranks of spiritual beings who were present in the atmos- phere and environment of Saturn, we will therefore select the Spirits of Form and be clear that they have gone through an evolution up to today, just as all beings go through an evolution. As man received his etheric body on the Sun, his astral body on the Moon, his ego on the Earth and has become more and more perfect, so have the Spirits of Form passed through their evolution.

These Spirits of Form had no physical body on Saturn, their lowest member was an etheric body which one can compare with the etheric body of man; thus we should have to think away completely the physical body in the Spirits of Form, and think of the lowest member of their being as the etheric body. Then these beings had an astral body, an ego, spirit-self or Manas, life spirit or Budhi, spirit man or Atma and an eighth member which is a stage higher than man can reach in the course of his evolution through the Earth's embodiments. These Spirits of Form therefore act externally on Saturn through their etheric body as man on Earth works externally through his physical body. They possess no hands through which they can work, no feet with which they can walk, for these are members of the physical body. But their etheric body manifests in such a way that they continuously ray in fructifying life-saps from the Saturn atmospheric mantle, which are of very rarefied matter. We can picture Saturn as we have described it, and from the environment—continuously and from all sides—fructifying life-saps streaming down like rain from the etheric bodies of the Spirits of Form. The nature of Saturn was such that it did not retain these fertilizing life-saps but rayed them back like a mirror. In this way arose the mirror pictures of Saturn of which I have spoken in earlier lectures, but now more exactly. You can picture the warmth substance of Saturn perpetually receiving the rays of the etheric body of the Spirits of Form and raying these back again. We can form a rough picture of it, if we remember how the rain drips from the clouds down to earth, collects in the earth and rises up again as misty vapors. We must not however imagine this as having an interval of time, but picture the process as a continuous one; the rank luxuriant life-saps stream in and are reflected, so that the rudimentary physical bodies appear like mirror-pictures. They actually consist of mirror-pictures. You can form an idea of what was present on Saturn as the physical germ of man, if you imagine a person standing before you and you look into his eye; you send your light into the eye of the other, and your picture comes back to you rayed out of his eye. So it was with the Spirits of Form in the environment of ancient Saturn. They sent their life-bestowing saps down into the warmth masses of Saturn and their own form, their likeness, was reflected; this mirror likeness was the first rudiments of the human physical body. Man was thus, even on ancient Saturn, in the most literal sense a likeness of his Godhead.

If we now go on to the Sun which arose out of old Saturn, the advance was made through the fact that the Spirits of Form no longer have need of an etheric or life-body; they give up the etheric body. They no longer ray down the life-giving saps, they relinquish their etheric body and in this way the first physical germs of man were permeated with an etheric body. The etheric body which the human beings received on the Sun was formed, to begin with, from the etheric body of the Spirits of Form,—a portion of the etheric body of the Spirits of Form. These celestial beings mirrored themselves in the warm Saturn, and through the fact that they brought a sacrifice and created pictures, they have gradually grown more independent and capable of the greatest deed, namely, to lay aside their etheric body in sacrifice and to permeate with their own life-force that which they first formed as picture. If you could endow with life the reflection which rays to you from the eye of your fellow man, make it independent, so that it had its own life and could step out of the eye, then you would have a deed which the Spirits of Form accomplished in the transition from ancient Saturn to the Sun. This was a significant advance for our cosmic evolution.

You know of course—I will just mention this here—that

all sagas and myths have a multiple meaning, and when we consider the true facts of world evolution in a spiritual sense, then the myths disclose their truth in a surprising way. This may be the case right here.

Let us look at the advance that took place from Saturn to Sun. On ancient Saturn the life-giving forces streamed in, were reflected and taken up again by the mantle, the atmosphere of Saturn. In the old Greek myth the warm globe of Saturn was called Gaea and the atmosphere Chronos. Now consider the myth: the life-giving forces of Chronos rayed in continually upon Gaea and were reflected and absorbed. It is Chronos continually swallowing his own children! One must feel the truth of such a myth; if it is not felt, one has not the right attitude to it. For just consider what it means: in hoary primitive ages of ancient Greece we find a myth that presents this truth to us in a wonderful picture. There is only one possible explanation of such a fact, namely, the most advanced individuals of mankind, who guided man's further development from the Mystery centres, had exactly the same knowledge of world evolution as we give out today in Theosophy. In the Ancient Mysteries they spoke of these things as we speak today; for the masses the truths were veiled in pictures and these pictures form what today we know as Mythology. In the face of such knowledge how extraordinary seem those people who believe that men have discovered truth only in the last forty years and that all knowledge possessed by men of earlier times is only childish fantasy. One must however describe it as a childish fantasy when it is emphasized again and again: "How marvellously advanced we are today!" That is the really childish picture!

So we advance from Saturn to Sun and consider the evolution of the Spirits of Form further. They have laid aside their etheric body, "exuded" it out of themselves and imparted it to the body of the Earth, inasmuch as the human bodies have permeated themselves with it. As the lowest member of their being they now have the astral body and their higher development means that they have not only one member above spirit-man or Atma, but a still further one. We must now describe their being as consisting of astral body, ego, spirit-self, life-spirit, spirit-man, an eighth and a ninth member which are beyond what man can attain in his completed seven-membered development. What do the Spirits of Form present as an "outside"?

The Spirits of Form have "trickled," so to speak, the life-rain down on to Saturn. On the Sun they manifest through instincts, desires and passions raying into the Sun, through all that is anchored in the astral body. If someone had sat there and looked out into cosmic space, he would not have seen lightning flash or heard thunder pealing, but round him in the astral light he would have perceived the passions of spiritual beings—everywhere, all around him, passions, and you must not at all imagine only lower passions. These passions and emotions now worked creatively on the planet from without. If we consider the myths further we see the creative Titans within our earthly evolution, the creative passions which worked from outside, from the spiritual airy circles of the Sun when this was a planet.

Now we advance to the Moon—the Sun is metamorphosed into the Moon. In the course of evolution this signifies that the Spirits of Form now lay aside their astral body also and that their lowest member is the ego. To describe their nature we should say: as the human being has the physical body for lowest member, so these Spirits of Form in the environment of the Moon have the ego as lowest member, then they have spirit-self, life-spirit, spirit-man, an eighth, ninth, and a tenth member. Thus they present their ego to the outer world. It is very remarkable, but so it is: they present externally pure 'I's, pure egos; they simply displayed sheer egos to the outside world. The whole activity in the surroundings of the Moon was as if one met with beings who revealed their whole character and individuality—and this was from the Moon's atmosphere inwards. Just imagine all your egos which are here in your physical bodies being suddenly freed from that and from etheric and astral body, imagine only your egos there as the lowest member, and that they could manifest themselves through space. Think of yourselves on the old Moon and your egos outside in the universe, but in such a way that they were embedded in the spiritual substances, only the lowest members of the Spirits of Form working in out of the air, then you will have a picture of how the Spirits of Form express themselves as sheer egos out of space. They have given up to the human beings the astral body which they still had on the Sun, so that on the Moon man now consisted of physical body, etheric body and astral body.

We will now picture the human being of Saturn who has the first rudiments of the physical body. We must visualize hovering above him beings who are the Spirits of Form and have an etheric body, astral body, I, spirit-self, life-spirit, spirit-man, to the eighth member. Now we must think of the next stage. In the Sun-human-being we have the physical body and the etheric body. The etheric body had been instilled into man by the Spirits of Form, keeping their astral body, so that they had their astral body, their I, up to the ninth member. Then we pass on to the Moon. We have man consisting of the physical, etheric, astral bodies. The astral body has been sacrificed to man by the Spirits of Form who then have as lowest member the I, and spirit-self, and so forth, up to the tenth member. All that we call 'man' has gradually flowed down out of the environment of the planet, has been put together, so to speak, from outside. All that is within was once outside, has entered into man from without.

Let us now follow evolution on the Earth itself: at the beginning man has the rudiments of his physical body, then his etheric, and astral bodies. The Spirits of Form came over from the Moon. Their lowest member is the I or ego. This they now sacrifice as well and with it fructify the human being in his rudimentary stage, so that the ego, as it appears on Earth, is a fertilizing force which streams out from the Spirits of Form, and these beings have now Spirit-Self or Manas as their lowest member.

If we wish to describe them we must say: Above us in the Earth's atmosphere there rule the Spirits of Form, their lowest member is Spirit-Self or Manas; in this they live and weave and they have sacrificed what they still possessed on the Moon—the ego working towards all sides, that 'trickled' down and fertilized the human being.

We will now follow the progress of man on the Earth itself. There one can point to the spot in man where the ego was trickled in, but today we will consider it only schematically. Man receives his ego. It comes in contact first of course with the astral body which surrounds him like an auric sheath, there the ego first flows in, interpenetrates the astral body. This takes place in what we call the Lemurian Age, in the middle of earthly evolution. In the Lemurian Age, in the course of long periods of time, different for each different human being, the ego drew into the astral body and fructified it. Let us picture this developing human being.

The physical body at that time did not consist of flesh and blood as it does today; it was a quite soft structure, even without cartilage, and was penetrated as if by magnetic currents. Then there was the etheric body and then the astral body which was fructified by the ego. We must imagine this fructification as being something like an indentation which occurred in the astral body, like a turned-in aperture. That is what actually took place, something like an opening arose at the top of the astral body through the inflowing of the ego, an opening as far as to the etheric body. (Fig. 1.) This was of great significance and produced an important result; the consequence was that the first dim perception of a physical outer world appeared. In earlier conditions man had perceived nothing but that which lived in him inwardly; he was as if hermetically sealed towards the outside. He was aware only of himself and what went on in him internally. Now for the first time there opened to him the sight of a physical outer world. But man was not yet quite independent, much was still regulated for him by other divine beings with whom he stood in connection. He could not immediately see all that was around him, as we do now; since only his astral body was opened he perceived only with that body. It was a quite dim clairvoyance, and when in this ancient primeval time the human being moved over the earth he perceived what was outside his body, he perceived if this were sympathetic or unsympathetic, beneficent or harmful. He perceived a color picture when he so moved about, a glaring-red, for instance, that arose as an auric color-picture, for it was his astral body that first opened. He knew that when a red picture appeared there was a being in the neighborhood that was dangerous to him. If a blue-red color met him, he knew that he could go towards it; thus he took his direction from these dim clairvoyant perceptions. He perceived only the soul elements, he could not perceive, for instance, what is present in the plants of today. He perceived only the soul-nature in the other human beings and in the animals, and the Group-souls, too. That was the first fertilizing with the ego.

The ego was gradually further developed and the fructifying element that entered the astral body began to permeate it more deeply so that the ego was increasingly present in the feelings of likes and dislikes. According as the ego expanded in this way in the astral body there arose what has been called in the book *Theosophy* the sentient soul. It is as if the fructifying ego spread its forces over the whole astral body, thereby producing the sentient soul. Here we still have to incorporate an important fact.

We have now seen a fairly normal advance of evolution. We have seen how the Spirits of Form on the Moon rayed in their lowest member, the ego, and how, when the Earth had arisen out of the Moon condition, they gave up the ego and fructified man with it. Now we know that certain beings on the Moon remained behind, beings who did not complete their development. What does that mean? It means that they had not advanced to the stage where they could let their ego stream out and fructify the human being. That they could not do. They still stood at the old Moon stage, when they worked with their ego into the atmosphere of the earth. There were laggard beings around man who worked on the earth as the Spirits of Form had done on the Moon. Man was surrounded in the earth's atmosphere by ego-beings who had not yet relinquished their egos. These beings now strove to accomplish on the earth what they had failed to do finally on the Moon. Man was thus exposed to influences that were not in the normal course of his evolution. These influences of the ego-spirits rayed into his astral body. While his astral body was molded through the in-trickling ego of the Spirits of Form, the ego-spirits, who were not at the stage of the Spirits of Form, rayed lower forces to him at the same time, lower than should have entered him in normal evolution. These lower forces brought it about that man divided into a higher and a lower part. Thus from the Spirits of Form an ego was instilled with the propensity to selflessness, whereas the laggard ego-spirits instilled into man the ego with the propensities towards selfishness, egotism. That is the ego which will still not free itself from instincts, desires, and passions. They press into the astral body and interpenetrate it—so that in man's astral body there is a twofold nature: selfless impulses that aspire to rise higher and those passions which are imbued with selfishness and have entered man through the influences of the ego-spirits and have anchored themselves in him.

Now we will further consider evolution itself. We have seen how the astral body has been entirely permeated by the force of the incoming ego. The next stage is when the etheric body too is seized by this force, so that here too a kind of aperture towards the outer world arises. To sketch this (Fig. 2) we must put in the middle a physical body, then an etheric body which is broken through and entirely filled with the force of the ego and then the astral body which is also entirely full of this force. So in the etheric body we now have a force desiring to expand; the etheric body opens to the outside world.

We have come in the formation of man practically into the first and second third of the Atlantean Age. There still existed an old clairvoyance which no longer saw in picture merely the beneficial and harmful, the sympathetic and unsympathetic, but a kind of living dream pictures arose before man which lasted a long time. For the etheric body is the bearer of memory and since these human beings had as yet no disturbance from the physical body, such pictures coming from outside were held for a long time. Memory at that time was an outstanding force of the soul. You can read in *The Akashic Record**) what man was at that time in respect of memory. There was not of course as yet complete observation of the external world, but a kind of dim clairvoyance. This was, however, more comprehensive than perception through the astral body. It caused everything to arise in mighty pictures, definitely formed, like a dream, but with a correspondence to the external objects, whereas formerly the pictures only served to guide man in taking his direction.

Now we advance to the last third of the Atlantean time. And now the physical body too is gripped by the force of the ego (Fig. 3). Rudiments of an indentation arise in the physical body, it becomes indented and around it we have the etheric and astral bodies. We will merely imagine the whole schematically now; in the course of succeeding lectures we shall get to know the realities. In a certain way, however, such a kind of indenting had appeared, the physical body took up the ego into itself. The point where the ego was taken in lies between the eyebrows, as I have often explained. The opening that comes about through the penetration of the ego into the physical body is to be thought of particularly as the opening of the physical senses. The ego presses through the eye, through the hearing—which

* See: Rudolf Steiner, *Cosmic Memory*, Rudolf Steiner Publications, Englewood, N.J.

is not merely an opening but a whole series of openings. All this takes place in the last third of Atlantean times and the human body was so transformed that it has become what it is today.

We call the etheric body as it was transformed at the beginning of the Atlantean Age the intellectual or mind soul and the transformed physical body we call the consciousness soul. So that what is described in my *Theosophy* as the position today, we have now followed as a consequence of evolution. You see here how things come about gradually.

After the physical body too is opened to the outside, man for the first time learnt to know the external world. And now begins the conscious transforming of the astral body. It was a more or less unconscious transformation before the beginnings of the consciousness soul. To picture this condition, we must think of it schematically like this: the astral body, etheric body and physical body opened, and through the fact that man comes in connection with the outside world he forms in himself an enclosure. This represents all that the ego develops in intercourse with the outer world, all that the ego "learns" through external contacts. Now imagine that the whole of what the ego develops in this way becomes greater and greater, and that this new structure, which has been gradually developed, lays itself round the astral body here. Although this is all schematic it corresponds to the actual process, and the new structure unites with man's astral body and in course of evolution transforms it into the human Manas or spirit-self. (Fig. 4.) Man is at work on this today, when through what he acquires in his intercourse with the external world he is transforming his astral body into Manas or spirit-self. We are in the midst of this process at the present time.

Since, however, the Spirits of Form have given up their ego, letting it trickle down into man, we are surrounded everywhere by these beings whose lowest member is of a Manasic nature, the spirit-self. If we want to seek in our surroundings for these Spirits of Form, for their lowest member, then we find it in that which we ourselves gradually develop as our fifth member. What we develop as human wisdom by which we must become wiser and wiser, that we should find manifested in our surroundings as the lowest member of the Spirits of Form. We have indeed often spoken of this. Let us look at what surrounds us, at what has been done by more exalted beings around us and in which we have taken no share. Let us look at what I have often mentioned, a piece of the thigh bone, in which the lattice work which goes to and fro is combined to such a wonderful scaffolding, that we must confess: Here with the minimum amount of material the maximum strength is attained! We see secreted in this structure what man will gradually learn—though it is impossible today—how to build bridge-scaffoldings through his engineering art that will be as wisely constructed as the thigh bones which carry the human upper body like pillars. The whole human body is thus wisely arranged, it is an expression of wisdom and when we go out into Nature this same wisdom meets us everywhere. Let us go, for example, to the dams which the beavers make. We see how the beavers collect at certain times of the year when the water has acquired a greater fall, in order to construct a dam in the water at a definite angle which will hold up the water and produce a new fall. Everywhere in our surroundings we find everything permeated with wisdom,—as we shall be permeated with it when we have developed Manas in full measure. The wisdom that we meet with everywhere belongs to the

Spirits of Form. As the physical body is our lowest member so is the wisdom which we find all around us the lowest member of the Spirits of Form, then they have Budhi, Atma, where we have our etheric and astral bodies and then they have the eighth, ninth, tenth, and eleventh members. We have to do here, as you see, with highly exalted beings to whom we look up; and when we see the wisdom in our surroundings, we see only the lowest member of these exalted beings. In comparison with these beings we are like a creature, a lower being, that creeps about on man and sees only the outside of his physical body. We creep about on the earth and see the wisdom, which for the Spirits of Form is what the physical body is for us. Such a being is a "creative spirit" as regards man, for this creative spirit has instilled his ego into him.

Precisely as we raise ourselves to Manas, so in the further course of evolution we shall someday acquire the life-spirit, Budhi, through the transforming of our etheric body. In our environment we have Manas or spirit-self as the wisdom impregnated into the world. That is the lowest member of the Spirits of Form, but there are also other beings linked with the earth whose lowest member is not our fifth, Manas, but our sixth, i.e. the life-spirit or Budhi. Around us is the atmosphere for beings whose lowest member—as member of higher beings—is equivalent to our life-spirit. And just as truly as at the beginning of the earthly evolution an external deed instilled the ego into man, so at a definite point of time there came the first impression and influence of the beings who little by little instil the full strength of Budhi. Two thousand years after the time in the ancient hoary past when the ego was poured down, there was still not much to be seen of such egos in the human bodies. That all came about gradually, only in the course of many millennia did the ego reach full manifestation. One must never imagine that the instilling of the ego was an event of which someone could say: "Nothing special happened; I do not acknowledge it, that is simply an event as others have been before!" If any particularly "enlightened" persons had lived on earth 2000 years after the instilling of the ego, and had perhaps represented the materialism of the time, they would have said: "Oh, there are certain among us who maintain that a special force has come down from heaven and brought all mankind forward. But that is a dualism of the worst kind, as Monists we must explain that that is something which was already there long ago!" These things appeared slowly and gradually.

Just as at the beginning of the Lemurian Age a powerful impulse forwards was given through the inflowing of the ego, which has later made possible the development of spirit-self or Manas, even so there has been an event of fundamental importance through which man will become capable with his whole being of developing not only Manas, but life-spirit or Budhi. And this event is the Deed on Golgotha. This event is the appearance of Christ on earth! It may be that some people will deny that to-day, but this event was just as much a force coming out of the environment as that other was. Thus we see that we grasp the evolution of the world from its spiritual aspect when we look into the depths of the world. We learn gradually not to look merely to a material existence, but we discover, wherever we look into cosmic space, spiritual beings and their deeds. Through what we call Theosophy we learn to know of these deeds, we live and weave and have our being within the spiritual beings and their deeds.

In our next lecture we will go more exactly into the human organism and indicate how the development has taken place, after today having dealt with it more schematically.

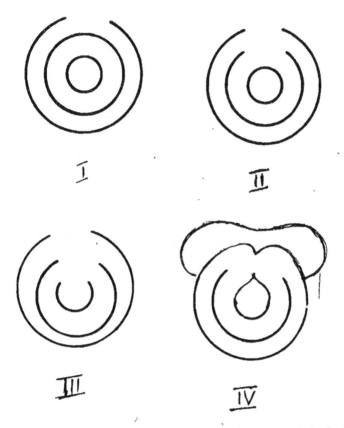

1. The astral body opens: dim clairvoyance, first third of the Atlantean Age.
2. The etheric body opens:
   second third of the Atlantean Age.
3. The physical body opens: the ego draws in. Formation of consciousness-soul. Last third of Atlantean Age.
4. The ego lays itself round the astral body. Today.

V

In THE last lecture we spoke in broad outline of the
development of the human being in connection with the
evolution of the cosmos. One can look at such things from
most varied points of view. For when we let our spiritual
gaze sweep back into the primeval past, then a no less rich
manifoldness of events is presented to us than in our immediate present, and one must not think that when one has
characterized phases of evolution with a few concepts and
ideas that one has fully grasped the matter or presented it
completely. It is necessary to characterize these past ages
too, and up to our present day, from the most varied aspects. We then become increasingly clear about them, but
must not let ourselves be misled by what appear here and
there to be contradictions.

Such apparent contradictions arise from the fact that
even to spiritual vision a matter can be seen from very
varied aspects. One can walk round a tree, for instance,
and make a picture of it from many sides. Each picture is
true and there may be a hundred of them. This is naturally
only a comparison, but in a certain respect it is perfectly
right for the ages of earthly evolution to be considered too
from many different aspects. Today we will consider the
evolution of our Earth in connection with the evolution
of mankind from a different point of view, and will pay
special attention to the human being himself. We will de-

scribe the processes which are presented in what we call the Akashic Record when we look back in spiritual vision to the past.

We have often related that our Earth before it became "Earth" went through a series of embodiments. First came the Saturn period, the Sun period, the Moon period, and only then our actual Earth period.

If we quite briefly look back to the time of ancient Saturn we remember that of the elements and bodily conditions which we find on the earth today, of the solid or earthy, the fluid or watery, the airy and the fiery, only warmth, fire, was present on ancient Saturn. We have the true picture of the first embodiment of the Earth if we realize the following: Saturn had nothing in it of the gaseous, the watery, nor of the earthy constituents. If you could have visited ancient Saturn, that is to say, supposing you could have been a modern human being at that time—as you neared old Saturn you would have found nothing of hardened, or watery, or any other substance, but a globe consisting purely of warmth; you would have gone into a sort of baking oven. You would have felt that you came into a different region of warmth. Thus old Saturn consisted purely of fire or warmth.

On the Sun, which was the second embodiment of our Earth, the warmth had already reached such a densification that we can speak of a gaseous or airy condition. The Moon condition showed a watery stage of our substances in its earlier period, and I have already told you how the Sun-substance went out of the old Moon and how then there suddenly came about a powerful densification of all Moon-beings.

The chief thing for us today is to be clearly conscious that at every later stage of evolution the earlier must in a certain way be recapitulated. So when we look back at the evolution of our Earth itself we have at the beginning a kind of Saturn stage, a repetition of the Saturn stage. Then we have a kind of Sun evolution, a repetition of the Sun stage, then a kind of Moon evolution, a repetition of the Moon stage, and only then really began the present embodiment of our Earth evolution. As our Earth came out of the Pralaya, the twilight condition which it passed through after being Moon, our Earth too was again only a ball of fire. I have given you a description of how the other planets had loosed themselves. Let us first hold fast to the fact that the Earth was purely a fiery ball containing nothing but warmth substance. Within this warmth ball of fire the human being was potentially already in existence. As the first rudiment of man was present on Saturn, so now in the recapitulation of the Saturn condition on the Earth, again man was present. There was no other kingdom. Man is the first-born of the Earth condition. At the beginning of our earthly evolution there was no plant kingdom, no animal kingdom, no mineral kingdom. Our Earth at the beginning of its evolution was in fact composed only of human bodies.

What then is the difference between the old Saturn condition and its recapitulation on Earth? There is a considerable difference, for the human bodies which then came forth, as fresh plants develop from seeds, had passed through the three earlier stages of evolution. Their formation was essentially more diverse, more complex, for all the forces which were at work in Saturn were present in this first Earth condition. Within it too were the old Sun and old Moon. They united at the beginning of Earth evolution forming again a single body, the forces of Saturn, Sun and Moon worked in it together. And so this first humanity at the beginning of Earth evolution was much more complex than the human being of Saturn. In Saturn all was undifferentiated—everything then was Saturn man. Now in the newly-arisen Earth, Saturn, Sun, and Moon worked together. Man arose in his first rudiments, although these rudiments were very complex.

When the Earth emerged and lifted itself, so to speak, out of the darkness of cosmic space, it was a space glowing with inner warmth, and living within it were the first forms of mankind as warmth-beings. When with clairvoyant sight you look back at what actually existed of man at that time you find at first these original human rudiments as if the whole warmth sphere had many, many currents in it. These currents go towards the surface of the newly-arisen Earth, sink into the surface, and form there masses warmer than the surroundings. The human being was distinct from the environment simply through the fact that one felt that certain spaces were warmer. It may be clearer for you to realize to what extent man was then in existence, if I record which of the human organs had been formed in its first rudiments at that time.

Think of a new-born child which still has a quite soft place on the top of the head. Imagine this place quite open, and imagine a warmth-current coming from outside into this opening. Think of the warmth-current not densely material in blood-streams, but in streams of force going down and forming a kind of centre where your own heart is and taking its course in separate arteries—not blood arteries, but force-arteries. There you have the first rudiments of warmth-man. Later on, in the progress of evolution, the human heart with its blood vessels arose from this rudimentary warmth-man. The blood circulation has arisen from it, and the organ which existed for a long time

75

in man's evolution and which later disappeared was a shining warmth-organ, though in its first rudiments. Much later in earthly evolution the human being still had such an organ. At the place still remaining soft in the head of an infant a kind of warmth-organ projected from man when as yet he was unable to see his surroundings. When he was still a sea-being and could not perceive in our present way, when he still swam about in the sea, he had to know of the temperature conditions, whether he might move towards a certain direction or not. He was made aware by this lantern-like organ whether he might go here or there. Man possessed this organ right into the third epoch, the Lemurian Age. I once told you that the legend of the Cyclops—the human being with the one eye—went back to this stage. It was no real eye and to describe it as an eye is not correct. It was a sort of warmth-organ which indicated the directions which might be taken. So we should have something like a goblet-shaped organ spreading out downwards to the first rudiments of the heart, and surrounded by something like prehensile arms, while up above one would have a sort of blood-organ. This was the appearance of the organ in the earliest periods.

Now in the course of the evolution of the Earth something very important entered. Matter, substance, became differentiated. The homogeneous warmth-matter was differentiated in such a way that air-matter arose while a part of the earlier warmth-matter remained. And here you must be aware of a law: you must be quite clear about it if you wish to consider these human beginnings in the course of evolution: Wherever the warmth-matter densifies to air, then at the same time light arises.—Warmth-matter is still dark, not permeated by light. But when a portion of the warmth in such a cosmic sphere condenses to gas or air, then a portion of this matter can let light come through. And so it was.

Now we have the Earth in the second stage of its evolution. (All other aspects go parallel with it.) We have now an Earth which consisted partly of warmth, partly of air, and shining inwardly. And all that takes place is expressed at the same time in the development of man. What was formerly merely a rudimentary warmth-organ now began actually to shine. The human being was like a kind of lantern, he shone. One need not find this particularly marvellous, it is no longer anything extraordinary. A few centuries ago one would have been amazed to hear of luminous beings, but there is no cause for amazement today. Natural science knows that down in the ocean depths, where it is impossible for a ray of light to penetrate, there are beings which shine, shedding their own light. And thus at that time the human being began to radiate light.

Now something extremely peculiar came about on this human formation, the rudiments were added for making use of the surrounding air. This was further developed later and the beginnings of a breathing process were formed. Thus we see a sort of breathing process added to the previous warmth process. It is important to be clear that with the deposit of air in the Earth the breathing process appeared, and that this in fact was the addition of air to the warmth-matter, permeating the warmth with little bubbles of air. This, however, is connected with something else, the effect of the light is there too and is manifested in the first beginnings of a nerve-system, an inner nerve-system. Not indeed a physical nerve-system, it is more a case of lines of force which have developed to densification. You must think of the whole as airy and only very fine air-currents can be there as lines of force. Thus we have now a rudimentary human being which in all fineness was still etherically a being of warmth and air and in which the first signs of a nervous system were shown. That was the stage of our earthly evolution when the Sun was still in the Earth. Imagine how this cosmic body appeared in universal space.

Imagine that someone looked across at this cosmic body from outside. All the beings which we have just described as the human beings radiated an individual light, and this light became the total light that shone out into the universe. If you could have examined the Saturn-condition you would have found that you could approach without seeing it; it could only be perceived through its warmth. But now you have to do with a Sun-body, inwardly warmed but sending its light out into space.

Now gradually came the time which I have described to you as the departure of the sun. All the higher beings who were connected with the sun and who gave the human beings the capacities of which we have just spoken, detached themselves, together with the finer substances. The sun went out. It no longer shone and spread out light, it went out of the earth.

So then we have a cosmic body which consisted of earth and moon, for the present moon was at that time still in the earth. And something very remarkable came about. Since all the finer forces had gone out with the sun, a very rapid—relatively rapid—densification resulted. What were earlier only lines of force took on a thicker form. And as the finer substances went away we see how the gaseous condition condensed to water. The whole body now consisted not only of fire and air but of water, too. The force of illumination had gone out with the departing sun and there was again darkness on the earth; the beings had kept for themselves inwardly only a portion of the light-force. This was an interesting stage of humanity's evolution. I have shown that the light laid the foundation of the nervous system. The nervous system is a creation of the light. In all your nerves you have the original streaming-in of the light. Now the light, the sun, went out into cosmic space and substance therefore densified very rapidly. It was not yet the same as the nerve-substance of today, but it was denser than before, it was no longer a fine etheric substance. And the important thing was this: formerly it shone outwards, now it became luminous inwardly. That means that man's first nerve-system had the power of creating inner light-pictures, visions; clairvoyant consciousness arose.

Thus the sun went out of the earth, left the earth without light, but the beings created an inner light. Formerly they had shone out to the light that shone towards them; now ·they had lost the power of shining. The earth was no longer sun; but their inner consciousness was illumined as today in sleep you illumine your consciousness with the whole world of dreams. This inner shining consciousness, however, was at that time infinitely more significant, more living. And now we come again to an important matter.

Just as light had arisen when the air arose, so now with the densification of air to water there likewise appeared a counterpart. As air is related to light, so is water related to sound, tone. Sound can of course pass through air, it sets the air vibrating and in that way it becomes audible. On the earth, however, sound arose—sound as such—side by side with the forming of water. And exactly as the action of light streamed through the air, so now the whole of the water to which the air had condensed was vibrated through and through by the currents of tone. The earth consisted then of warmth, air, water. The parts of the earth which had become fluid were in particular permeated by sphere-harmonies, by tones which streamed into the earth from the universe in every possible harmony. The result of this action of sound in the water-element was a very, very important one. You must picture to yourselves that in this original water, this fluid-earthly water, were contained all those substances which exist separately today as metals, minerals, and so on. It is extremely interesting to look back with spiritual vision to this ancient time and see how most varied shapes were formed. Tone created forms in the water. It was a quite amazing period of our earth's evolution. Something took place then on the grandest scale similar to what happens when you strew fine sand on a metal plate and stroke the plate with a violin bow. The Chladni sound-figures are formed and you know of course what regularly-shaped figures and formations appear. Thus the instreaming music from cosmic space gives rise to most manifold forms and figures, and the substances dissolved in the water which were themselves watery, they listened to the cosmic music and arranged themselves in conformity to it. The most important formation of the dance of the substances to cosmic music is albumen, protoplasm, the foundation of all living growth. Materialists may think as they will of the mechanical construction of albumen from oxygen, nitrogen, carbon, and so on; the original protoplasm was formed of cosmic substance that had been formed from the harmonies of cosmic music. And thus the substances in the living were organized according to the world-music. The albuminous substance, protoplasm, now surrounded and entered into the fine structures, penetrating everything. The water, congealed to albumen according to cosmic tone, took its course along the lines which I described as lines of warmth and gradually passed over into blood formation. The congealed water established itself as albumen in the lines of the nerves. And in the first place the albumen formed a kind of sheath, cartilaginous gluten, one might say, as a protection from outside. All this actually took form from the dance of substances to the music of the spheres.

This was all in existence before there was a single cell. The cell is not the origin of the organism, but what I have just described. The origin of the organism is spirit, first existing as warmth, then indicated more in lines of force, then what arose from the sphere-harmonies through the arrangement of substances, depositing itself in these lines of force, and only relatively later as the final formation the cell arose. The cell as the last excretion had to be born from a living creature. Organisms have never formed themselves out of cells, but the cell has first formed itself from the living. The anatomical is always a sequel of combination.

We have all this at the beginning of the condition of the earth when it still contained the moon after the departure of the sun. But as long as the moon remained in the earth there was an increasing hardening of the albuminous formation, and the state that I have described to you as mummifying would have resulted if the coarsest substances and beings had not left the earth. The last developed portion of the human creature at that time were the nerves that went to the sense organs. But the sense organs had not yet opened. They had been formed from within outwards but as yet they were not open. And now the moon went out together with the coarsest substances. The consequence was that the human being could then gradually pass over to a higher condition. His senses were opened, the two heavenly bodies were now outside and could hold a mutual balance. Whereas they built up man as long as they were united with the earth, they now worked in from outside; they opened his senses and made him a seeing, hearing being as he appears to us today. The departure of the moon was practically in the middle of the ancient Lemurian Age. We then have a human being who had not yet opened his sense-organs but who had a powerful gift of clairvoyance. I have already described how he could fill his consciousness with most varied color and warmth phenomena from within, all of which had real worth and significance, yet he could not perceive the objects in space. That only began after the moon had left the earth.

If you consider this brief sketch which I have given you of the ancient earth-evolution you will see that present man actually took his starting point as earthly being from the heart outwards. The heart was of course not such an organ as it is today; that only developed much later, but the rudiments of the heart proceeded from the fire-element. Then were added the breathing system born of the air, the nerve-system born of the light. Then came the protoplasmic material which inserted itself into the organs and formed the whole to living matter through the cosmic tones congealing the fluid substances. In the final period, when the moon substance was still present in the earth, densification to the condition of earthy solidness came about. It was actually only shortly before the departure of the moon that what today we call the mineral kingdom arose, that is, the earth element out of the fluid element. Albumen is in fact a state midway between the solid and the fluid. But the earthy, the solid, actually arose only in the latest period. Why was that? It arose because under the influence of densification—for everything was involved in a continuous process of condensation—the elements themselves had become more and more material. Think for a moment of the beginning of Earth-evolution. What did the warmth-matter do there? It gave you for your bodily nature that which now pulsates in your blood. You must not think that when we speak of the earliest warmth condition of the Earth we are speaking of such a warmth as arises when you strike a match. That is mineral-fire and mineral-warmth. We are speaking of the fire and warmth that pulsates in your blood; that is living warmth. In fact there is not only the mineral warmth that arises externally in space, but there is a very different one, a living warmth which you have in yourselves. That was present at the beginning of the Earth and from it were formed the first rudiments of man. But even this living warmth gradually became lifeless with the continuous densification. That was connected with the densifying process which came about when the sun went out and the moon was united with the earth. The mineral warmth first appeared as the process of combustion.

Here we come to something important which I ask you particularly to note. It is true that at the beginning we can talk of a condition of fire, of warmth, but we cannot speak actually of combustion. That would not be correct. We should speak only of what we feel pulsing warmly in our own blood. The warmth that comes from an external mineral combustion appeared only when the sun had gone out and the earth was alone with the moon. And through the combustion process, formerly not there at all, a substance was separated off within the earth-mass which is described in occultism as "ash." When you burn something it gives rise to ash. The ash embedded itself in the structure of the earth when earth and moon were united. Evolution had now got so far that through the cosmic tone which pressed in and brought the substances to dance, the protoplasmic masses inserted themselves. There were beings where fine protoplasmic substances had earlier become organized along the lines of force, this protoplasm being similar in outer formation to the formation of the present albumen. There were also denser substances which acted as a protection, surrounding the beings like a sort of glutinous sheath.

What is lacking in these beings? The hard bone substance! If I may express myself popularly, everything was still more of a glutinous mass, and anything of a mineral nature was entirely absent from them up to the time I have now described to you. Now you must think how different these beings were. You have nothing in your physical body today that is not permeated by mineral substance. The human body as it is today has arisen only relatively late. It consists not only of bones but of muscles and blood, mineral substance has embedded itself in everything. Think the mineral substance away, think of the whole Earth and its beings as yet without mineral substance—and then by a combustion process the deposit of ash, ash of the most varied mineral substances. In the human beings, therefore, which up to then had in fact only arrived at a glutinous density, ash constituents became embedded in every direction. And the beings absorbed the ash as formerly they had taken up the albumen and organized themselves in their own way—took up the mineral element from the dense bones to the fluid blood.

You can easily form an idea of what was embedded—all that remains behind as ash when the body is burnt or decays. What actually remains behind as ash is what originated the

84

last of all. Everything in you that does not remain behind as ash was there previously; it stored up the ash in itself. One who observantly regards the ash derived from a moldering corpse must say to himself: that is the mineral substance in me, which was last of all absorbed by what existed previously. Thus the mineral arose last in the course of the earth's development and the other kingdoms stored it up in themselves, having previously consisted entirely of other substances.

We can ask what was the reason of this incorporation of the ash. We carry ash within us the whole time, only it is distributed and is left behind when our corpse is burnt or decays. How did the ash press into the lines which were filled by albuminous substance?

We have seen that originally there was fire and the rudiments of the heart were formed from it. Then the rudimentary stage of breathing was produced by the air, light entered and formed the rudiments of the nerves. Then came sound and produced the living substance by causing the materials to dance. But what caused the ash-element, the mineral, to stream into this substance?

What pressed ash into the human bodies was now henceforth *thought,* which made the sound, the tone, into the *word.* Even in Atlantean times, when everything was immersed in mist, what the human being spoke was not the only articulated language, but man understood the speech of the rustling trees, the rippling springs and founts. All that today is articulated language and all that was expressed in it, formed the dance; tone, the musical element in it, formed the materials into living substance. The sense, the significance, of the word pressed into this living substance the ash that formed out of the combustion process. And to the degree in which the bony system gradually condensed towards the end of the Atlantean Age man was penetrated by thoughts, by self-consciousness. His intellect dawned and he became increasingly a self-conscious being. The things that exist in us are created from outside: First, the rudiments which develop into the human heart; second, our nervous system with the rudiments of breathing; third, the glandular organs, arising out of the living; fourth, the bony structure, permeated by ash; finally, man becomes a self-conscious being. Such was the course of evolution within our own Earth-embodiment, and we have now arrived in our description nearly at the end of the Atlantean time.

If you compare this with our earlier studies, you will see that what is active last was always there first; for that which pressed into matter as "Word" was there the first of all. That which has given man his ego was there at the very beginning. If you try clearly to understand what has been said today you can also very readily find the facts again in the first sentences of St. John's Gospel. In one of our next lectures we must show how our studies which have swept out into cosmic space are beautifully presented in the Gospel of St. John and also in the first sentences of Genesis. All these things are regained for us when we consider the course of evolution. One thing, however, will plainly emerge: When we look at the facts, our human evolution is seen to be very different from what materialistic fantasy imagines. Materialists think that man has been produced from coarse matter and that his spiritual faculties have been developed out of it.

You see now that the actual mission of earthly evolution, that in which Love comes to expression in man, was laid down first in what we possessed as warmth organ, which emerged the first of all. Before anything organic, Spirit was there in the form of lines of force, then came the incorporation of the organic under the wonder-working of world music. Then only was the whole impregnated with mineral substance, solid matter, through the Word or thought. The densest arises the latest. Man develops out of the Spirit, and this is seen too if we study the course of earthly evolution. Man has his origin and primal state—as every genuine study of the universe has always shown—not in matter but in Spirit. Matter embedded itself in the human being later than the spiritual forces, and this becomes increasingly clear from what we have been studying.

VI

IF ANYONE present at the last lecture given here has been carefully thinking it over, and remembering how certain stages previously passed through are recapitulated at a later stage, how, for instance, on our Earth a Saturn stage, a Sun, a Moon stage gradually emerges and only then our earthly condition fully develops, he could feel urged to make the following remarks.

He could say: In various earlier lectures it has been stated that on Saturn the first physical rudiments of man went through something like a sort of senses-system, as though the first Saturn rudiments had consisted of primitive elementary sense-organs; then on the Sun a glandular system developed: on the Moon a nervous system and on our Earth all this was recapitulated. But how does that tally with what was said in the last lecture, that is, that the first to appear on Earth was the first rudiments of the blood-system, a kind of warmth-man? Then it was said that there was a condensation to an airy-state and light arose, on the one hand a sort of air-system was added which later became our present breathing system, while the warmth-system was transformed to the later blood-system, and under the influence of the light a kind of inwardly perceiving nerve-system was formed. It was further described how that was all still in a rarefied etheric condition, was then filled out with a kind of albumen which, under the influence of cosmic sound and tone, arranged itself into the different substances.

If I admit—the objector might say—that the glandular system only began with the depositing of this organic substance, then the first thing on the Earth would be a kind of warmth-system which formed the rudiments of the blood-system, and a kind of nerve-system present in fine etheric lines of force; then the glandular system would arise which in a certain respect was already organically substantial, and last of all the mineral element would be deposited as was described in the last lecture. If the successive conditions of Saturn, Sun, Moon have appeared and these conditions are then recapitulated on the Earth, it is strange that the senses-system is not the first to re-appear, then a glandular system, a nerve-system, and finally a blood-system. Yet last time just the reverse was described: first blood, then nerves, glands, and finally the solid deposits which, as it was emphasized, first open the senses towards the outer world. The objector might say: This recapitulation-principle works out very badly since the order which has been given is just the reverse of what one might expect if a really literal repetition took place.

It must be admitted that if someone wished to describe the succeeding conditions as a simple repetition of the foregoing, he would probably give a description that was the very opposite of what had really existed. For the intellect would conclude that in an automatic way first the Earth would recapitulate what had taken place on Saturn, then what had happened on the Sun, then on the Moon, and that only then the blood-system arose. I have often emphasized that as a rule in occultism one always goes wrong and can make terrible mistakes unless one describes out of the occult facts and does not trust oneself to mere intellect or any purely logical conclusions. For if one follows the evolution of Saturn, Sun, Moon in the Akashic Record it is a fact that one must say a kind of senses-system was planned on Saturn, a glandular system on the Sun, a nervous system on the Moon, and with the Earth the blood was added. If one follows up the occult facts further, then one finds that actually on the Earth first a kind of blood-system appears, then a glandular system, a nervous system, and only then arises what appears as the senses-system in the form suited to Earth-conditions. Thus if one speaks of recapitulations, according to the actual facts one must speak of a reversed recapitulation. What has been shown in earlier lectures and what was shown in the last springs from no speculation, but from the actual facts and these display just such a reversal, which makes the recapitulation all the more complicated.

We must not, however, content ourselves with the idea that we have to do with a mere reversal. Just as the blood-system in its first rudiments appeared on the Earth as a kind of warmth-man, as I described last time, yet at the same time it was really a kind of sense-system. It was in fact a system of warmth and perception. The human being was, so to say, wholly a blood or warmth-man. He was not permeated by the substance of blood, but etheric warmth-lines of force penetrated him, and these etheric warmth-force-lines out of which the blood-system later arose were in the first rudiments distinctly a kind of sense-system. It was the first rudiments of a sense-system, and the nerve-and-light system was at first a kind of glandular system, and the later glandular system which was organized was really only able to arise because the other systems, the blood- and nerve-systems, now incorporated, advanced in their development. This advance occurred in the following way: Whereas the nervous system developed as a kind of glandular system, something of the blood remained behind as the later rudiments of the blood. But as well during the second stage the blood-system itself changed to a kind of nerve-system; and when that was achieved and, in the third stage, the glandular system was incorporated, the two earlier systems again changed, so that in fact the blood-system advanced a degree and the nerve-system also a degree. Changes and transformations are continually taking place. Evolution is very complicated and one may not rest content with the idea of the reversed recapitulation. For the "reversal" is again only partial: the blood-system is a sense-system which is transformed later, and it is the same with the nerve-system, and so on.

So you see that what has gone before and enabled the human being to reach his present height is certainly not an easy-going matter for the intellect. The point is with patience and perseverance to familiarize oneself with this complicated course of evolution. However, this is merely a kind of introduction which I wanted to give for those who have been studiously dwelling again upon what was said in the last lecture.

A quite different task shall concern us today—that of considering man and his evolution on Earth from an entirely different standpoint, so that this human being shall come before us with increasing clarity. If, with this in mind, we look back once more to the previous embodiment of our Earth, the ancient Moon, then we remember that the human being had physical body, etheric body, astral body, but not yet a personal ego as he now possesses on Earth. If we now examine the consciousness of such a Moon-man we find it was radically different from that of a human being of today. The consciousness of man today is really expressed in what one could call "personality." With this word much is said in the characterization of the Earth-man, for there was no "personality" on the old Moon. We have seen how this personality has been formed gradually on the Earth and how in ancient times man still felt himself much more as a member of a whole number of others who belonged to one another. Even if we go back not at all far in the regions where we ourselves are living, yes, even if we go back to the first Christian centuries, we shall still find there the last echoes of an ancient consciousness. The ancient member of the Cherusci, the Sugambri, Heruli, Bructeri, did not feel himself to the same extent a personality as does the man of today, he felt himself one of his tribe. And when he said "I," that signified something entirely different from what it means today. If a modern man says "I," he means the entity of his personality, that which, so to speak, is enclosed within his skin. At that time men felt with regard to their tribe as a limb feels on our organism. He felt himself in the first place as a member of the Sugambri, Heruli, Bructeri, Cherusci, and only in the second place a personal "I." You will have a better understanding of many ancient conditions if you bear in mind this radical alteration in personality, if you realize, for instance, that certain forms of family revenge, tribal revenge, are to be explained completely by the common consciousness of the tribe, a kind of group-soul-consciousness. And if we go still farther back to the classical Old Testament time, the time of the Jewish people, we know that the individual Jew felt absolutely that he was a member of the whole Jewish people. We know that when he said "I" he did not feel himself as representative of his ego, but felt the blood of the whole folk as it had streamed down in the generations since the Father Abraham: "I and the Father Abraham are one." Each member of the race felt that this

92

was what gave him his value and position. He felt the group-soul in the blood right back to the Father Abraham. And if we go still farther back, into the earliest ages of the Earth, we find the group-soul element still more clearly expressed. The individual had a memory of what his forefathers had done, back to the earliest ancestor. The memory of the descendants went back for hundreds of years. In our day, in normal circumstances a man no longer remembers what his father has done, unless he has seen it. He no longer remembers what his ancestors have experienced. In ancient times man had a memory not only of what he had himself experienced, but also of the experiences of the ancestors with whom he was of common blood, not because he knew of it but because memory was continued beyond birth. And we know that the great age attributed to the Patriarchs, to Adam and the succeeding ancestors of the Jewish people, meant originally nothing but the length of memory, how far one remembered in the ancestral tree. Why did Adam live so long? Why did the other Patriarchs live so long? Because one was not designating the single personality, but remembered past generations as one remembers one's youth today. That was denoted by a common expression, personality did not come into question at all. A man remembered not only what he had gone through in childhood, but what his father, his grandfather had experienced in childhood, and so on through the centuries, and one compressed the contents of this memory into a unity and called it—let us say—"Adam" or "Noah," and so on. In primitive ages the separated personality had nothing of the value that it has now; memory reached beyond father, mother, grandfather, and so on, and as far as it reached one used a common name. That seems clumsy and fantastic to the present-day materialistic conception of the world, yet it must be affirmed

93

from the depths of the facts by a fundamental psychology which knows how to reckon with the facts.

On our Earth therefore man had a kind of group-consciousness connected with his group-soul. If we were to go back to the old Moon where the human being had not a restricted ego of this sort embedded in the group-consciousness, but where he had no ego at all, where he still consisted of physical body, etheric body, astral body, we should find that this old Moon-consciousness was not a smaller one but embraced immensely great groups—that in fact all-embracing group-souls were the basis of the human race on the Moon. These group-souls who, so to speak, set individual Moon-men on to the Moon merely as their limbs, were wise souls. We have, as you know, also described the animal group-souls on the Earth and have also found wisdom as their out-standing characteristic. These Moon group-souls have implanted in our planet's previous embodiment the wisdom which we know today and which we so much wonder at and admire. And when today we are amazed how every bone, how heart and brain, how every plant leaf, is permeated and imbued with wisdom, then we know that the wisdom of the group-souls trickled down from the atmosphere of the old Moon—as clouds today let the rain trickle down—and membered itself into all the beings. These received it as a propensity and brought it out again when they appeared on the Earth after the Pralaya. Thus there were present on the Moon all-embracing group-souls filled with wisdom.

Now if we were to seek on the old Moon for a quality which we find today on Earth in ever-increasing measure as evolution goes forward, we should not find it existing in the Moon beings. This quality is love, the impulse which leads beings together of their own free will. Love is the mission of our earthly planet. Hence in occultism we call the Moon the "Cosmos of Wisdom" and the Earth the "Cosmos of Love." As we today, standing on the Earth, wonder at the wisdom embedded in it, so one day the beings of Jupiter will stand before beings from which love will stream forth to them in fragrance. Love, as it were, will issue in taste and fragrance from all the surrounding beings. Just as wisdom shines towards us on the Earth, so on Jupiter there will come fragrantly towards the Jupiter beings that which is evolving here on Earth as love—from the purely sex-love to Spinoza's "Divine Love." It will send out perfume as plants send out their various aromas. Thus will the grades of love stream out as the perfume ascending out of the cosmos which, as successor to our Earth, we have named Jupiter. Thus in the course of evolution conditions alter, and whenever an advance occurs in evolution the beings advance too; they who are united with the stages of planetary evolution are ever advancing to higher stages. The human beings living on the Earth today are the instruments of the evolution of love. For the animal kingdom has developed forms of love which have stayed behind as laggard forms; and in so far as love appears among the animals, a simple reflection would show that it is all pre-stages of human love, of the love that is continually being spiritualized. As man is the instrument for the evolution of love on Earth, so when he has evolved to Jupiter he will be capable of receiving a still higher quality. So too those beings who "trickled" down wisdom from the periphery of the Moon became capable of a higher evolution when the Moon became Earth; they ascended higher. The beings who at that time were able to let wisdom trickle into the Moon-beings were in fact those who were so advanced at the time when the sun withdrew from the earth that they went out with the sun and made it their scene of action. The beings who on the Moon were spirits of wisdom—the wisdom that trickled down— were not the Spirits of Wisdom which have been so named in connection with Saturn—these spirits, or at any rate a great number of them, chose the sun as their theatre. Only the Being whom one designates Yahve or Jehovah, who had reached full maturity on the Moon, became the Lord of Form on the Earth, the Regent of the Moon forces. But we have already spoken of other beings who did not complete their development on the Moon, who remained, so to speak, midway between human and divine existence. We have characterized them in manifold ways. We have indicated that the sun at a certain stage of its evolution put Venus and Mercury out of itself in order to give these beings a theatre which was suited to them. We have also spoken of beings who have taken part in man's progressive development and who, as Venus and Mercury beings, have been the great teachers of humanity in the Mysteries. Today we will en- large this picture from another standpoint.

We have already pointed out that if the forces and beings which left the earth when the sun withdrew had remained united with the earth as they were originally, then man would have been obliged to develop at a tempo too rapid for him to endure. He would never have reached his evolution if the Spirits of Wisdom had been bound up with the earth as they were on the Moon. They had to remove to a dis- tance and work from outside if man was to have the right speed in his development. Otherwise, no sooner was he born than he would have become old, he would go through his development at too rapid a tempo. I can make that clear to you in another way.

The spirits who had evolved up to the sun existence are not at all interested in man's gradual, slow development of his spiritual nature during his bodily existence, during childhood, youth, maturity, old age. They have an interest only in the perfected development of spirituality. If they had remained in connection with the earth, human bodies in a certain way would have been stunted, burnt up. Without maturing the fruits won from an earthly existence the spirit would have gone towards a rapid evolution and the human being would have lost all that he can learn on the earth. Above all, the imprinting of Love into the evolution of the cosmos would have remained concealed. In order that love might develop on earth the body had first to be developed at a primitive stage. Love had to be inaugurated in the lowest form as sex-love, in order to rise through the various stages and finally, when the perfected Earth has reached its last epochs, to be imprinted into man as pure, spiritual love. All lower love is schooling for the higher love. Earthly man is to develop love in himself, so that at the end of his evolution he may be able to give it back to the Earth, for all that is developed in the microcosm is in the end poured into the macrocosm. The wisdom which streamed into the Moon-men shines towards the earth-man as the wisdom which permeates his structure. The love which by degrees is implanted in man during the Earth period will waft fragrantly towards the Jupiter beings out of the whole realm of Jupiter. This is the path that the various cosmic forces must take.

Thus the starting point of our Earth's mission—the impressing of Love—was in a certain way confronting the two following tendencies. The Spirits of Wisdom, the creators of wisdom, who on the Moon had streamed wisdom into the kingdoms of the Earth, were on the Earth, as such, uninterested in the physical bodily nature of man. As Spirits of Wisdom they were uninterested in it, and being interested only in wisdom they gave up the special Earth mission to the "Spirits of Love." These are another rank and as Spirits of Love they too had been able to go through their own evolution for a time on the sun. In this way we have a twofold tendency in the evolution of the Earth: an instreaming of love which, as it were, appears for the first time, and an instreaming of wisdom which works from outside, since the spirits pre-eminently interested in wisdom have withdrawn to the sun. It is very important to grasp correctly this co-operation of the Spirits of Wisdom and the Spirits of Love, for it expresses an infinitely important contrast. If I now try to put into human language what this contrast expresses, it is that the Spirits of Wisdom wholly relinquished to the Spirits of Love man between birth and death and the way in which he develops, and took for themselves the control of the "individuality" which goes through the various "personalities" in the course of reincarnations. If you picture man in his totality you have here the analysis which shows under what two powers he stands in cosmic rulership. What man is between birth and death, what he develops in himself while living in the body, what really makes him, so to speak, an entity who stands on his two feet on the earth, that is placed under the authority of the Spirits of Love. What weaves through the personalities as the enduring individuality, is born with the man, dies, is born again, again dies, and so on, that stands in a certain respect under the authority of the Spirits of Wisdom. But you must not treat this mechanically and say: So you state that the human individuality stands under the influence of the Spirits of Wisdom and the human personality under the influence of the Spirits of Love.—If one were to stereotype things it would only lead to nonsense. For concepts are only valid if we understand them in their relativity and know

98

that every concept has two sides. Only if you were of the opinion that this one life between birth and death were meaningless for all the following lives then you might stereotype it like that. But you must keep in mind what I have always emphasized, namely, that the fruits of each separate earthly life, that is, the fruits of all that has been gained under the influence of the Spirits of Love stream into the whole of evolution and thus into what is guided by the Spirits of Wisdom. On the other hand you must be clear that everything in the human body, right up to the astral body (we have already described how experiences made on the earth must be transformed) proceeds under the power of the Spirits of Wisdom, so thus again the Spirits of Wisdom work on man's being since he has a physical body, an etheric and an astral body. And because whatever man as personality develops under the element of love is enduring for his individuality, the Spirits of Love work again into what is developed in the single human life via the Spirits of Wisdom Thus they work together. Then the rulership of these Spirits is again divided inasmuch as all that is personality stands directly under the control of love, and all that happens between birth and death stands indirectly under the element of wisdom.

Thus we see how man's personality and his individuality are within two different tendencies and currents. That is important for the following reason. If the Spirits of Wisdom who are meant now, had, so to speak, arrogated authority to themselves, then that exuberant, vigorous development would have come about which one could also describe by saying that in a single incarnation man would have gone through, pressed together, all possible perfectings from all incarnations. That which the Spirits of Wisdom were to give, however, became distributed among 'all man's successive earthly incarnations. That is expressed in occultism quite definitely by saying: Had the Spirits of Wisdom remained in evolution man would rapidly have developed to spirituality, burning himself up bodily throughout evolution. But the Spirits of Wisdom refrained from bringing man to such a violent development. They went away from the earth in order to circle round it—in order to regulate and modify the time-periods which would otherwise have rushed past so vehemently. One therefore says in occultism that these Spirits of Wisdom became the "Spirits of the Rotation of Times." The successive incarnations of man were regulated in the successive revolutions of time which were again regulated through the course of the stars. The Spirits of Wisdom became Spirits of the Rotation of Times. They would have been able to lift man away from the earth by their wisdom-filled power, but then he would have had to forgo the maturing of fruits which can only take place in the course of time. The fruits of love, of earthly experience, would not have been gained. Those secrets which beings must possess and hide in their hearts in order to mature the fruits of love, of Earth's experience, were veiled from these Spirits of the Rotation of Time. Hence it has been recorded: "They veiled their faces before the Mystical Lamb." For the "Mystical Lamb" is the Sun-Spirit Who holds the secret of lifting not only the spirits away from the earth but of redeeming the bodies, spiritualizing them, after many incarnations have been passed through. The possessor of the Love-Mystery is the Sun-Spirit Whom we call the Christ, and since He has an interest not only in the individuality, but directly in each single personality of the earth, we call Him the "Great Sacrifice of the Earth" or the "Mystical Lamb."

Thus certain Spirits became the Spirits of the Rotation

of Times and regulated the successive incarnations. The Christ became the centre, the focus, in so far as the single personalities were to be sanctified and purified. All that man can bring as fruit out of the single personality into the individuality he achieves through having a connection with the Christ Being. Looking towards, feeling oneself united with the Christ purifies and ennobles the personality. If Earth's evolution had taken its course without the appearing of the Christ then the human body—if we speak in a comprehensive sense—would have remained evil; it would have had to unite with the earth and fall a prey to materiality for ever.

If, however, the Spirits of Wisdom had not renounced the immediate spiritualizing of man at the beginning of Earth's evolution one of the following two courses could have been taken: Either the Spirits of Wisdom, at the very beginning of earthly evolution—in the Lemurian age— would have torn man away out of the body, led him to a rapid spiritual evolution and quickly consumed his body, in which case the Earth could never fulfill its mission;—or, on the other hand, they could have said: We do not wish for that, we want the human body to develop fully, but we ourselves have no interest in it. We will relinquish it therefore to the Late-born, to Jehovah; he is the Lord of Form—and man would have been dried up, mummified. The body of man would have remained united to the earth, it would never have been spiritualized.

Neither of these ways was chosen, but in order to form a balance between the Spirits of Wisdom and the Last-born of the old Moon, the Lord of Form, who was the point of departure for the creation of the present moon, a central situation was created. This mid-way solution prepared for the appearance of Christ Who is exalted above wisdom, before Whom the Spirits of Wisdom veil their countenance in humility, and Who will redeem men if they permeate themselves more and more with His Spirit. And when the earth itself reaches the point where man will have spiritualized himself fully, then a dried-up ball will not fall out of evolution, but through what he has been able to draw out of evolution man will lead his increasingly ennobled human form to complete spiritualization. And we see how human beings are spiritualized. If we were to see the original human bodies of the Lemurian Age—which I should never describe in a public lecture—we should find that they represented the extreme limit of ugliness, and men became more and more ennobled as love increasingly purified them. But man will evolve even beyond the present human countenance. To-day we are in the 5th race. In the 6th race the external physiognomy of man's countenance will show his inner goodness, the inner state of his soul. Man will have then quite a different physiognomy; by the outer form one will recognize how good, how noble he is, one will see by his countenance what qualities lie within his soul. Increasingly will the physiognomy receive the imprint of the nobility and goodness contained in the soul, until at the end of the earth-condition man's bodily nature will be entirely permeated by spirit and will stand out in complete relief from those who have remained attached to materiality and will bear the image of evil on their countenance. That is what will come. It is called the "last crisis" and must be described as "Spiritualization" or, as it is popularly called, the "Resurrection of the Flesh." One must only understand these things in the true sense as given by occultism, then they cannot be attacked. Enlightened circles will not be able in any case to understand that matter could someday become quite different from matter. What could be called in the best sense of the word the "madness of materiality" will never be able to imagine that matter could one day be spiritualized—that is, that someday something will come about which one calls spiritualization, the Resurrection of the Body, of the Flesh.

But this is how things are, and this is the course of earthly evolution, and thus comes about the meaning of earthly evolution and the place of the Christ within earthly evolution. If we were merely to look at all we have been considering today, then we should have a peculiar picture of the evolution of our Earth. Such a picture would show that the scales were in fact held between the Spirits of Form and the Spirits who have become the Spirits of the Rotation of Time, the actual Spirits of Light. Through the fact that the Christ from the time of the Mystery of Golgotha has to guide earthly evolution, they would be in the position of equilibrium and a continuous ascent would result. But the matter is again not so simple. We know that Spirits have remained behind—Spirits who had not attained the full maturity of the development of wisdom, and who therefore had no interest in relinquishing their authority on the instreaming of love. These Spirits wanted to work on and let wisdom continue to stream in. They did so, and hence their work on earth has not been entirely unfruitful. They have brought men to liberation. If the Christ-Principle has brought love, so have these Spirits, whom we call Luciferic Spirits, brought men freedom, the freedom of the personality. Even the staying behind of certain Spirits has its very good side, and everything, whether advance or staying back, is of divine nature. So there were Spirits of the Rotation of Time who guided progressive incarnations—that which passes as individuality through all the different incarnations; and there were Spirits of Love under the guidance of the Christ-Principle who so prepare this individuality that the personality can little by little go over into a Kingdom of Love. If we would characterize the great ideal that hovers before us as a Kingdom of Love we can do so in the following way.

In the widest circles today the radical error is still circulated that the well-being of a single personality is possible without the well-being of all others on the earth. Although men may not admit that directly, yet in practice our modern life is based on the fact that the individual lives at the cost of others and it is a widespread belief that the welfare of the one is independent of the welfare of the others. Future evolution will bring about the full community of the spirit, that is, on Jupiter the belief will begin to prevail that there is no health and happiness of the one without the health and happiness of all the rest, and indeed to an equal degree. Christianity prepares this conception and it is there in order to prepare it. A community arose at first through the love that was bound to the blood, and in this way sheer egotism was overcome. The mission of Christianity is now to kindle in man the love that is no longer bound to the blood—that is, that men learn to find the pure love, where the well-being of the one cannot possibly be conceived without the well-being of the other. Anything else is no real Christianity. In this way we can characterize the evolution of man to a higher stage. But the advance of evolution to such a stage occurs in cycles, not in continuity. You can make these cycles clear to yourself through simple reflection.

You see how a civilization arises in the first epoch of the Post-Atlantean Age, reaches its culmination and must again decline, how it attains its highest point in the flight from materiality but how it must recede because it has sought its culture on the ground of the non-acknowledgment of matter. You then see how a new cycle enters with the old Persian civilization, how it conquers the earth through the acknowledgment of matter, at all events as a power striving against man, which man subdues through his labor; again this culture reaches its culmination and sinks into decadence. But a new civilization ascends, the Egyptian-Chaldean-Assyrian-Babylonian, which no longer merely acknowledges matter, but penetrates it with human intelligence—where the orbits of the stars are investigated, where buildings are erected in accordance with star-wisdom, laid out in accordance with the laws of geometry. Matter is no longer an opposing power but is recast and remoulded to the spiritual. And after the Egyptian-Chaldean-Assyrian-Babylonian culture has fallen into decay, we go on further to the Greco-Latin culture, where in Greek art man has so transformed matter that he has formed his own image in it. It had never been the case before that, as in Greek sculpture, Greek architecture and drama, the human being imprinted his own image into matter. And with Roman civilization we see added the legal idea of the personality. It is only a quite perverted scholarship that says the legal concept had already existed earlier—a rational man can see that at a glance. The Law-book of Hammurabi is entirely different from what was created in Rome as jurisprudence. That is a genuine Roman product, for jurisprudence emerged where the personality created its image in law too; in law man is placed entirely on his own personality. One should study and compare the testament of the Roman Law with what one finds in the Law-book of Hammurabi, where man's personality was definitely given its place in a theocracy. The "Roman citizen" was a new element in the evolutionary cycle of mankind. And there will be a new cycle when men have fully grasped what comes forward today as Theosophy. We see how each cycle in civilization reaches its peak and again declines and how each new cycle has the task of carrying civilization further.

The firm position of balance gives man the certainty that he can be redeemed from the Earth, and the struggling upwards and the striving away is the struggle for actual freedom, which the Luciferic Spirits have imprinted into mankind. Thus the Christ-Principle and the Luciferic Spirits work together in world evolution and determine the conditions of civilization. It is of no consequence that in early Christian centuries the Luciferic principle was excluded and men were referred to the Christ-Principle alone. Humanity will surely come again to their attainment of freedom by complete devotion to the Christ-Principle; for the Christ-Principle is so all-embracing that he alone can grasp it who seeks to encompass it on the level of the loftiest wisdom. Let us glance back into pre-Christian times. We find religions existing there as preparation for Christianity. We see religions, it is true, among the Indians and the Persians but religions suited to the particular people out of which they have been born. They are national, tribal, racial religions, appearing with the coloring out of which they have arisen, limited inwardly, because in a certain way they still proceed from the group-souls and are bound up with them. With the Christian religion an element entered humanity's evolution which is the true element of earthly evolution. Christianity from the beginning at once broke through the principles of all earlier religions. It sharply set itself against the sentence "I and the Father Abraham are one." It opposed in the first place the idea that one can feel oneself a unity with something that is only a human *group*. On the other hand the soul that dwells in every personality must be able to feel one with the eternal Ground of the World Whom we call the "Father" and Who dwells in every soul, and this is expressed in the sentence: "I and the Father are one." And in contrast to the Old Testament which begins with the words: "In the beginning was the Light," Christianity sets the New Testament words: "In the primal beginning was the Word." With this was given one of the greatest advances in humanity's evolution. For in referring to the light that arose, one speaks, in so far as one can speak of light, of something externally visible. The old records contain a Genesis that establishes the physical as a manifestation of the light. The "Word," however, is what issues from the inner nature of the being, and before any manifestation of light had appeared there existed in man "what was, what is, and what is to come," namely, man's inmost being. In the Primal Beginning was not the Light, but the Word. The Gospel of St. John is not a document that may be placed side by side with the others; it expands the others from the temporal to the eternal.

So Christianity stands there, not as a religion which might be a national religion but, if it is rightly understood, as a religion of mankind. In that the Christian feels himself one with the "Father," soul confronts soul, no matter to what people or nation it belongs. All divisions must fall away under the influences of Christianity, and the Jupiter condition must be prepared under the influence of this principle. Christianity therefore has begun as a religion, for humanity was founded on religion. Yet religion must be replaced by wisdom, by knowledge. In so far as religion rests upon faith and is not inflamed with the fire of full knowledge it is something that must be replaced in the course of humanity's progress. And whereas formerly man had to believe before he could come to knowledge, in the future full knowledge will shine with light and man will know and thence ascend to the recognition of the highest spiritual worlds. From religion mankind evolves to wisdom, glowed through by love. First wisdom, then love, then wisdom glowed through by love.

Now we can ask: If religion is to merge into knowledge, if man is no longer given religion according to the old form, namely, that according to his faith he is directed to the wisdom that guides evolution—will then Christianity too no longer exist? There will be no religion that is founded on mere faith. Christianity will remain; in its origins it was religion—but Christianity is greater than all religion! That is Rosicrucian wisdom. The religious principle of Christianity as it originated was more all-embracing than the religious principle of any other religion. But Christianity is still greater than the religious principle itself. When the outer coverings of faith fall away it will be in wisdom-form. It can entirely strip off the sheaths of faith and become wisdom-religion, and spiritual science will help to prepare men for this. Men will be able to live without the old forms of religion and faith, but they will not be able to live without Christianity, for Christianity is greater than all religion. Christianity exists for the purpose of breaking through all forms of religion, and that which fills men as Christianity will still exist when human souls have grown beyond all mere religious life.

VII

I SHOULD like to speak to you today about something
that to a certain extent falls out of the series of our present
course of lectures. In another respect, however, it forms a
supplement to them, recapitulating much that has been
said and shedding more light on it.

We know indeed that man has only reached his present
condition in the course of a long evolution, that he has developed to his present heights through different planetary
stages. We know too that he will lift himself to higher
stages of evolution in the future. Now we are also aware
that when the human being was still in quite a dull state of
consciousness on ancient Saturn, there were beings already
in existence who stood as high as man stands today.
There were beings too who at that time stood far higher
than man stands today. We also know that there are beings
today who have already attained a stage of evolution which
man will only attain in the future. So we can look up to
hierarchies—as they are called in occultism—of beings set
over man whose various ranks are ranged one above the
other.

The beings who stand next above man are called in
esoteric Christian terminology "Angels," Angeloi. The
Angels are therefore beings who in the Moon-evolution, the
planetary forerunner of our Earth, had already attained human consciousness and who stand today one stage higher

than humanity. In the Jupiter-evolution man will himself have the consciousness which is possessed today by the beings whom we call Angels, Angeloi. This then is the first stage of beings standing above man, and from certain other connections we know of the subsequent stages.

Passing upwards beyond the Angels we have the Archangels, Archangeloi; then the rank of the "Original Forces" whom we also call Archai; and then the "Revelations" or Powers, Exusiai; the so-called Mights or Dynameis; the Dominions or Kyriotetes; the Thrones; the Cherubim, and the Seraphim. Then only, beyond the Seraphim, should we speak of what in the Christian sense, one calls the actual "Godhead." Genuine occultism, true spiritual science, cannot share the usual trivial notion that man can look up direct to the highest Divinity; we have the whole ladder of Beings whom we call Angels, Archangels, and so on, standing between. In a certain respect it is a sign of indolence to say—as we can often hear today—"Well, why do we need the whole succession of beings? Man can quite well come to a direct relationship to the Godhead." The student of spiritual science cannot share this indolence, for the beings are absolutely real. And today we will say something of their qualities and their tasks.

We will first try to form an idea of the nature of the Angels. We shall most easily form an idea of their consciousness if we think of the physical consciousness of man and how it includes the four kingdoms of nature. He can perceive mineral beings, plant beings, animal beings and the human kingdom itself. We can therefore describe the human consciousness as one having for its contents these four kingdoms perceptible to the outer senses. Everything that man perceives through the senses, no matter what it is, belongs to one of these four kingdoms. If we now ask: What is the consciousness of the Angels? we receive as answer: In a certain respect it is a higher consciousness since it does not reach down to the mineral kingdom; the Angel's consciousness does not reach down to where the stonès, rocks, minerals are. On the other hand it includes plant, animal and human beings together with its own kingdom of Angels which there plays the same rôle as the human kingdom does for us. We can say then that the Angels are also aware consciously of four kingdoms, the kingdoms of plant, animal, man and the kingdom of the Angels.

That is the peculiarity of the Angel beings: they have no physical body and therefore no organs of the physical body such as eyes, ears, and so on. Hence they do not perceive the physical world. As their lowest being they have the etheric body and hence have a certain relationship with the plants. Their consciousness can descend as low as the plants and they can perceive them. On the other hand, where there is mineral they perceive a hollow space—just as during the devachanic condition, man, as we described, will also perceive as a hollow the space filled up here on earth by a mineral. So that wherever the physical kingdom is here, the Angels perceive a hollow space. On the other hand, their consciousness projects up to where as yet man's consciousness does not reach.

But we know too that men bear a certain relationship to each other; there are those who lead and those who are led. I wish to allude only to children and grown-up teachers: children must be guided until they are as mature as the teachers. Men are growing in their present development into the Jupiter consciousness, which will be similar to what the Angels possess today. The Angels today are therefore actually the leaders of men, their guides, preparing them, and there exists an intimate connection between what gradually develops in man and the task of these Angel beings. What then is forming in man during the rest of his earth existence? It is something of which we have often spoken. We have said that man has a physical body, an etheric body, an astral body and an ego and that he is now occupied in transforming his astral body so that it gradually becomes spirit-self. He is working on his other members as well, but the essential task of earthly existence consists in the full development of the spirit-self. The Angels have developed it already, they had developed it when Earth-existence began, and thus the Angels in the hierarchies of evolution are the spirits which guide this task of man—the transforming of the astral body into the spirit-self.

Now we ask how they do this.—Let us remember here what happens after a man's death and how he has round him at first what we have called the memory panorama of the just completed life. This lasts for two or three days, it differs somewhat for individual persons. It lasts as a rule for about the length of time that the person could hold out without sleep. Different people vary very much in this: one is accustomed to sleep after every twelve hours and then his eyes close; another on the contrary could keep awake for four to five days. The memory-tableau lasts as long as the person can keep himself from sleeping. Then the etheric body dissolves and only an extract of it remains—the life-fruit of the past life. This is taken with him for the whole of the time that follows, is incorporated into his being and forms the basis for the upbuilding of the physical body in the next incarnation. He is enabled to build up his next body more perfectly, because he can make use of the fruits of his past life. Thus man has this life-essence and forms his next body out of it in the life that follows.

Now we know too that man not only forms this body but that in Devachan he is by no means inactive. It would be a false idea to think that man had only to occupy himself with himself. The world is not built up on such egotism. In every situation of life the world requires man to share in working on the earth and during his stay in Devachan he shares in work upon the earth's surface. We are aware of the fact that the ground on which we stand today looked quite different a few centuries ago; the earth is continually transformed. At the time when Christ Jesus walked upon earth there were mighty forests here, there were quite other plants and animals. Thus the face of the earth is continuously changed. Just as men labor with physical forces in building cities and so on, so from Devachan they work with those forces which transform the physiognomy of the Earth together with the plant and animal kingdoms. In a new incarnation therefore man meets a ground that presents quite a different picture; he always experiences something new. It is not for nothing that man is born into a new incarnation; he is to experience something new. Man contributes to the transformation of the Earth, but he cannot do it without guidance. He cannot determine the succeeding incarnations, for then he would not need to experience first what is to happen in the future. And the beings who guide man's work of transforming the earth with the forces of Devachan, who create the harmony between the different human individuals and the evolution of the earth as it corresponds to them, these spiritual Beings are the Angels. On the stones, on the solid earthly crust they cannot work, for their consciousness does not extend to the mineral, but it reaches down to the plant kingdom which the earth bears. There they can work, not indeed creatively, but transformingly. Such an Angel being works in fact with every human individual, guiding him in his task of developing the spirit-self in the astral body. In a part of Christian doctrine it speaks of man's Guardian Angel and that is a conception completely corresponding to reality. They are the beings who create the harmony between the human individual and the course of earthly evolution until man will have advanced so far at the end of Earth's evolution that he can release his Angel. He will then himself have the consciousness of an Angel.

Now you will readily understand that the Archangels have a consciousness that no longer reaches down to the plant kingdom but only to the animal kingdom. The plants, so to speak, do not exist for them, the plant kingdom is too subordinate, too insignificant. They still have points of contact with the animal kingdom and can perceive it. They have no etheric body, the astral body is the lowest member of their being. The animal has an astral body and hence the Archangels work in the astral bodies of the animals. In addition they perceive the human kingdom, the kingdom of the Angels and their own kingdom. The Archangel kingdom is that to which they say "I," as is for man the human "I." These beings too have an important mission, and since they have a consciousness two stages higher than man, you can understand that the mission must be a very lofty one. The consciousness of the Archangels is so high that they have fully perfected the life-spirit, Budhi, and they can therefore guide and lead in earthly evolution from an insight corresponding to the life-spirit. This is shown in the fact that the Archangels are leaders of whole peoples; what one calls the folk spirit, the common spirit of the people or folk, is in reality one of the Archangels. You will now find it comprehensible that those peoples who were still conscious of such a spiritual connection, did not look up direct to the highest

Being, but that they turned their gaze to the Beings nearest to them, who directed and led them.

Let us take the old Hebrew people. They revered as the highest God, Yahve or Jehovah. But for them Yahve belonged to the rank of the Revelations. He was a sublime Being whom they acknowledged as their God. They said, however: He who directs and leads us as the actual archmessenger of Jehovah is "Michael," one of the Archangels—his name means "the one who stands before God." In ancient Hebrew he was also called the "Countenance of God," because when a member of the Old Covenant looked up to God he felt that Michael stood before Him and was the expression of His being as the human countenance is the expression of man's being. He was therefore called literally the Countenance of God.

When one speaks in occultism of the folk spirit one does not speak of an incomprehensible being difficult to grasp. When in our materialistic age people speak of the folk spirit they really mean nothing, they mean by it an abstract external combination of the characteristics of a folk In reality there is a spiritual representative, an Archangel, who leads and directs the people as a whole. This Being reaches down into the animal world, and this was felt by the peoples, they felt it out of their instinct. The one folk dwelt here, the other there, and according to the different regions they occupied they had to make use of such and such animals. They felt instinctively that this was allotted to them by their folkspirit. This spirit worked as far as the animal world, so that the ancient Egyptians, who experienced this very clearly, said: When we consider plant development, then the Angel is working into it; when we consider the animals, these are apportioned to us by the guiding spirit of the whole people. They therefore saw the power which supplied the animals to them as a sacred power and the way in which they treated the animals was an expression of this consciousness. They did not speak of Archangels but they had the same feeling about it, and it was this feeling that the Egyptians united with the animal worship. Moreover, where there was a consciousness of this spiritual connection, these spirits were not represented by pictures of earthly animals, though with animal images, as for instance the Sphinx, winged beasts, and so forth, which you find in the various images of the peoples. It was as if the guiding Archangels shone in, and you can see portrayed in the different animal groups the esoteric expression of the ruling Archangels. Many of the Egyptian idols were based on the conception that the Archangel, the guiding spirit of the people, reached down as far as the animals. This is the special task of the Archangels; there is, however, still another task.

The names "Uriel," "Gabriel," "Michael," are still known to the modern consciousness, but as a legend from the far past, and you need only look in the Book of Enoch to find the names of yet other Archangels. So, for instance, there is "Phanuel," an important Archangel who has not only the task of guiding some people or nation, but another task too. We are aware that initiation consists of the fact that man strives upwards to an ever higher consciousness, and that even now in the course of earthly evolution he is ascending to an ever higher consciousness. Now the people in the Mystery centres knew well that here too guiding, leading forces were necessary. They therefore brought those who were to be initiated under the protection of the Archangel Phanuel. He was the protector who was called upon by the candidate for initiation.

Other spiritual beings of this rank have yet other tasks. So, for example, the whole course of world evolution is based upon a sum of forces which are guided by certain beings. Thus there is an Archangel, earlier called "Surakiel," whose task it is to eradicate particularly wide-spread vices of a city or a whole district and to transform them into virtues. To one who knows this connection it is plain that what is called in general by the abstract word "Providence" is really guided. If one has undertaken the study of the spiritual worlds one should not be satisfied with general abstractions, but go into these details. For the highest beings of whom man can form any idea guide the course of world-evolution through such intermediate beings as we have just considered. These can be denoted as the various tasks of the Archangels.

Now we come to the rank of the "Original Forces." They are still more lofty beings whose consciousness no longer descends to the animals. When the initiate lifts himself to intercourse with the Original Forces, he does not impart to them out of his human consciousness information about the animal forms on the earth. For their consciousness reaches down only to man; then they know the kingdom of the Angels, the kingdom of the Archangels and their own kingdom. To themselves they say "I," and human beings are the lowest hierarchy which they perceive. For the Original Forces man is the lowest kingdom, just as the stone, the mineral, is the lowest for man. We see from this that they guide the progress of humanity from a very lofty height. People here and there have an inkling that something exists as a kind of "Spirit of the Age," that differs according to the different epochs. We have often spoken here of the Spirit of the Epochs. We have said, for example, that in the first culture-epoch of the Post-Atlantean Age, that of the ancient Indian people, the Spirit of the Epoch consisted in the fact that men looked back to Atlantean times when they dimly perceived higher kingdoms around them. So the Yoga system arose, by means of which they sought to rise into the higher worlds. The physical plane of external reality had little value for them; it was maya, illusion. It will seem strange to you, but it is actually true, that if the ancient Indian civilization, with its lack of interest in the physical plane, had continued, there would never have been railways, telephones, and such things as exist in the physical world today. For it would not have seemed at all important to occupy oneself seriously with physical laws in order to people the world with all that today represents the achievements of civilization.

Then came the Spirit of the Persian epoch, and man learnt through him to know matter as an opposing element which he must work upon. He united himself with the good Spirit, Ormuzd, against the Spirit of matter, Ahriman. But the Persian had an interest in the physical plane. Then comes the Spirit of that epoch which found expression, on the one hand, in the civilizations of Babylon, Assyria, Chaldea, and on the other hand of Egypt. Human science was founded; it was sought through geometry to make the earth suited to man. One sought to know the meaning of the motion of the stars in astrology, astronomy, and one arranged earthly affairs in conformity with this motion. Eygptian social life was especially directed according to the passage of the stars. What was read there as the secrets of the stars was the basis of human conduct. The ancient Indian sought the way to the Gods by turning his attention completely away from outer reality; the Egyptian studied the laws which rule in order to find how the will and spirit of the Gods were brought to expression in the laws of external nature. That was again a different epoch. So you have for each epoch a definite spirit, and the evolution of the Earth comes about through one Spirit of the Epochs being relieved by another —that is the case in detail. People rise to the conception of Ages, but they do not know that behind this whole progress of the Ages, Spirits of the Epochs stand, nor do they know that to bring to expression the Spirit of their epoch they are only the instruments here on earth of Spirits standing behind them. Just think of Giordano Bruno. If Giordano Bruno had been born in the 8th century, he would not have become what he became in the period ruled by the Epochal Spirit whose expression he then became. He was the instrument of the Time-Spirit, and the same applies to other outstanding human beings. And conversely, the Epochal Spirit would not have been able to find such an expression as it found in Giordano Bruno, if Giordano Bruno had been born in the 8th century. By such things we see how men are the instruments of the Epochal Spirits who are the guiding beings of the great epochs and also of the Spirits of the "meanings and conceptions" of the smaller epochs. They are the Original Forces, they extend their consciousness down to man. They have no directing influence over what brings man together with other nature-kingdoms, for their consciousness does not reach the animal kingdom. How men conduct their lives according to the spirit of the time, how they found states, found sciences, cultivate their fields —everything of human origin, the progress of civilization from beginning to end stands under the guidance of the Original Forces. They lead man in so far as he has to do with others.

I have drawn your attention at various times to the fact that certain beings from each spiritual hierarchy stay behind, they have not risen as high as the others, but have stood still, so to speak, in world-evolution. You will be able to realize that there are beings who should have risen during the Moon-evolution to the rank of the Revelations or Powers, but who have only reached the Original Forces. They are different from those who have ascended to that stage in the normal course of evolution. Hence there are on earth Original Forces who are really immature Powers. We are now learning to know from another aspect many things of which we have heard already. Concealed behind the Original Forces, therefore, are some who could actually be Powers, and among the Original Forces who have really no right to be there is that being whom one is right in calling "Satan"—Satan, the "Unlawful Prince of this World." This is a truth, however, only to those who look at things from the aspect of spiritual science. The Lawful Prince is one of the "Powers," Yahve or Jehovah; the unlawful belongs to the ranks of the Original Forces. He expresses himself by continually bringing confusion into man's relation to the Time-Spirit, by bringing men to contradict the Epochal Spirit. That is the true nature of the Spirit who is also called the "Spirit of Darkness," or the Unlawful Prince of our Earth, he who claims to be the actual guide and leader of men. You will now grasp what a deep meaning lies in the fact that the Christ appeared in order through His mission to throw a light upon the whole succeeding evolution, and that He must wage war against this Unlawful Prince of this World. The very deepest wisdom lies behind what is expressed in this remarkable passage in the Gospel.

It stands to reason that a certain view is held not among materialists alone but also by people who are haunted by old conceptions which they misunderstand—for Satan has for a long time been spoken of somewhat scornfully! And even people who are ready to acknowledge the other spiritual beings are not willing to concede reality to Satan; they deny him. This dates back to the Middle Ages when men had very curious views on Satan. They admitted that he was actually a backward Spirit of the rank of the Powers. But where are the Spirits of the Powers? They express themselves in what is revealed in the world as spirit. Satan was called a Spirit of Darkness; people thought: Darkness is a negation of light, light is real, but darkness is not real—and they made that apply spiritually. They ascribed reality to the Spirits who manifest in light, but to Satan who manifests in darkness they denied reality. That is just about as clever as if someone who has listened to a physicist were to say: Cold is only a lack of warmth, it is not real in itself; if we make the warmth less and less, it gets colder and colder, however much warmth we take away; cold is not a reality —so do not let us think of winter! But in spite of cold's being only a negation of warmth, it can nevertheless very well be felt when there is no heating—so is Satan very well a reality even if he is only the negation of light.

We have now raised ourselves to very lofty Spirits, and we come next to the hierarchy who are called "Revelations," Exusiai. To them, for instance, belongs the being whom we have come to know in other connections as Yahve or Jehovah, together with his companions, the Elohim. The Spirits of Light belong to the order of the Powers or Revelations. We know that Yahve had six companions who separated off the sun. Yahve himself went with the moon which reflected the sun's light to the earth, but he is a companion of the other Elohim. If you now try to determine the consciousness of the Revelations on the analogy of what has gone before, you will realize that they do not concern themselves about the individual. Individual human beings are guided by the Angels, Archangels, Original Forces, up to those we have called Epochal Spirits. The whole structure in which man is embedded, the guidance of the planet and what occurs on it is the affair of the Revelations or Powers. For the whole present evolution of humanity could not have gone on without, on the one hand, the accelerating sun forces, and, on the other, the hindering moon forces. The Revelations or Powers have nothing to do with separate men but with groups of men. They guide the external powers and beings who give the planet its configuration and whom man needs in order that he may go through his evolution.

And so finally we look up to a lofty Being Who surpasses all that we have just described, the Christ Being Himself. Christ brings something to earth which is not concerned with the individual man, but with the guidance of all mankind. And to the Christ man must find his way himself; for it is only the Original Forces who constrain man to find them; to the Christ he must come of his own free will.

Thus we have formed some conception of the lowest ranks of the hierarchies set above man, the Angels, Archangels, and a slight idea too of the Original Forces and Powers. Only with a faint divining could we look up to a still higher Being, the Christ. On another opportunity we can consider what is to be said about the Thrones and so on. Today I wished to relate something of the spiritual structure into which man is interwoven, in so far as Angels, Archangels, Original Forces, and Powers participate in it.

VIII

IT WAS promised, when last we met for study, that a few things should be said for more advanced theosophists now that our Group had developed to this point. This expression 'advanced theosophists,' however, was not meant to imply any special theoretical knowledge of theosophical teachings. We can understand what is meant if we realize that taking part in the life of a theosophical Group has a definite effect on the soul, even though for a time it may be merely a period of waiting. During this life in a Group one not only acquires concepts and ideas concerning the nature of man, of the higher worlds, of evolution, etc., but far more than anyone is aware of one absorbs a sum of perceptions and feelings which are different from those that one brought with one as a newcomer to Theosophy. These perceptions and feelings are particularly connected with the ability to listen quietly and calmly and accept descriptions with a certain inner credence without looking on them as fantastic dreams. Before coming into touch with the theosophical world-conception one would probably have laughed and made merry over such ideas, and most certainly the majority of our contemporaries would make merry over them. This sum of feelings and sensations to which we gradually accustom ourselves is far more important than the details of theosophical teachings and theories. For, little by little, we actually become different through acquiring these feelings towards those

123

other worlds which are continuously pulsing through our world imperceptibly to our senses. People who have such feelings, who take this attitude to these other worlds, are those who in this case may be called "advanced theosophists." Thus an appeal is made to your heart, your feeling nature, and not to your theoretical knowledge. What the heart and feelings have absorbed constitutes the advancement we need if we are to accept freely and without prejudice the statements contained in recent lectures and in a certain way in the lecture to be given today.

If we were to talk in general abstract theories to give as little offense as possible to the sound human intelligence, we should only be deceiving ourselves. We should not have the real will to unlock that world which must gradually be unlocked by means of the Theosophical Movement.

We shall today make the acquaintance of beings who may be said to be among us, if we regard ourselves as spiritual beings, but to whom we have so far paid little attention in our studies. We have, as you know, always set man in the centre of our world conception, as the microcosm. To understand man and his evolution, however, we have been giving most attention to other beings, to higher spiritual beings who formerly played that part in our Earth evolution which is played today by man. We have seen that before our Earth entered on its present stage, it was what we have become accustomed to call the old Moon, and we know that certain spiritual beings who today stand higher than man were then passing through their human stage, although under different conditions.

` We have learnt that beings who are today two stages higher than man, the Fire Spirits, went through their human stage on the old Sun, and we have further learnt that the Asuras went through the human stage on Old Saturn.

Their qualities, good as well as evil, stand far above or below those of man. Thus in the course of time we have reviewed a whole series of beings who participate in the whole development of our life and nature. We have come to know beings to whom in a certain respect we must look up; and one who can observe clairvoyantly finds a significant distinction between them and man. You know that we differentiate various members of man's nature. We apportion to him a bodily nature—the physical body, etheric body, astral body—and, distinct from the body, a soul-nature—sentient soul, intellectual soul, consciousness soul—and thirdly, a spirit which is only in the initial stages of evolution. In the future phases of our planet man will bring it to a higher development.

When we examine the human being we therefore find him consisting of three parts, a bodily, a soul, and a spiritual part, which broadly speaking make up the threefold being of man. If we now look up from man to the higher beings of whom we have just spoken we may say that they differ from man by not having developed the coarse body. Those beings, for instance, whom we call Lunar Pitris, or Angels in Christian esotericism, possess no coarse bodily nature perceptible to the senses. They passed through the stage of humanity on the Moon and have now ascended higher. Such a coarse corporeal nature as man's cannot be attributed to them. On the other hand they have already developed the higher members of the spirit not yet possessed by man, so that we can say that they are spirit and soul, in contrast to man, who is a three-membered being —spirit, soul, body.

Thus, we have been occupying ourselves principally with cosmic beings who stand above man and have spirit and soul. For the occult observer, however, still other beings exist in the world, and although in the modern phase of human development they are largely concealed they nevertheless play a part in evolution. There are beings which clairvoyant sight cannot recognize as spiritual, for what we are accustomed to call spirit in man cannot be discovered in them: they consist essentially of body and soul.

Now from our previous studies you know a whole group of such beings, that is, the animals. They have body and soul. We know, however, that the animals are connected with their so-called group ego, and that this is itself of a spiritual nature. In the single animal standing before us in the physical world we have indeed a being possessing only body and soul, but it is continued, as it were, towards the higher worlds and linked to spirituality. I have often used a certain comparison in respect of the animal group ego : if there were a partition here and I stretched my fingers through it without your seeing me, but only the ten fingers, you would yet say that the fingers must come from someone who is invisible to you. It is just the same with the group egos; they are invisible and concealed for physical perception, but they exist nevertheless. The animal belongs to a group and the various animal groups are connected with the group egos above. It is therefore only when we refer to the single animal here on the physical plane that we can say animals have body and soul. What we see has a continuation into the astral.

But other beings exist which are no longer visible to the physical senses, beings possessing body and soul. In various occult teachings they are often called elemental spirits. To call them elemental spirits shows the greatest possible ineptitude, for it is just spirit that they do not possess. It is better to call them elemental beings, and we shall see shortly why their bodies are not visible. In the meantime let us accept as a kind of definition that such beings consist of body and soul. Their existence is of course denied in our enlightened age, for man in his present phase of development cannot see them; one who wishes to see them must have progressed to a certain degree of clairvoyant consciousness. The fact that a thing is not perceptible does not mean, however, that it is not active in our world. The activity of these beings of body and soul plays very definitely into our world. What they do can very well be seen, but not the doers themselves.

Now our first concern is to gain as far as is possible without definite perception some idea of these elemental beings which take various forms and occupy the spiritual realm that has received us all. They are also spoken of as nature-spirits; in fact, they have been given many different names. The name, however, does not matter; what is necessary is that we create a certain concept of them. And here already comes an appeal to your advanced feelings and perceptions. I should like to relate quite simply and plainly how such beings show themselves to clairvoyant sight.

There are beings that can be seen with clairvoyant vision at many spots in the depths of the earth, especially places little touched by living growths, places, for instance, in a mine which have always been of a mineral nature. If you dig into metallic or stony ground you find beings which manifest at first in remarkable fashion—it is as if something were to scatter us. They seem able to crouch close together in vast numbers, and when the earth is laid open they appear to burst asunder. The important point is that they do not fly apart into a certain number but that in their own bodily nature they become larger. Even when they reach their greatest size, they are still always small creatures in comparison with men. The enlightened man knows nothing of them. People, however, who have preserved a certain nature-sense, i.e. the old clairvoyant forces which everyone once possessed and which had to be lost with the acquisition of objective consciousness, could tell you all sorts of things about such beings. Many names have been given to them, such as goblins, gnomes, and so forth. Apart from the fact that their body is invisible, they differ essentially from man in as much as one could never reasonably attribute to them any kind of moral responsibility. What one calls moral responsibility in man is entirely lacking in them; what they do, they do automatically, and at the same time it is not at all unlike what the human intellect, intelligence, does. They possess what one calls wit in the highest degree and anyone coming into touch with them can observe good proofs of this. Their nature prompts them to play all sorts of tricks on man, as every miner can tell you who has still preserved something of a healthy nature-sense—not so much the miners in coal mines as those in metal mines.

The different members of these beings can be investigated by occult means just as in the case of man when we distinguish his members as physical body, etheric body, astral body, and ego and what is to evolve from them as spirit-self, life-spirit, and spirit-man. In his present phase of development man consists essentially of the four members first named, so that we can say that his highest member is the ego or 'I' and the lowest is the physical body.

But now we should succumb to delusion if we imagined quite abstractly that the physical body had nothing to do with man's ego. In man's physical body we have the instrument for the human ego. We have seen that the human body is a very complicated organization. In all essentials the ego has its physical instrument in the blood, the astral body in the nerve-system, the etheric body in the glandular system, the physical body in the physical organs working purely mechanically. We must picture to ourselves that all the human inner experience that goes on in the astral body has its material expression in the nerve system, and all that goes on in the etheric body finds its material expression in the glandular system, the instrument of the etheric body. Thus the physical body presents, as it were, an image of the four-fold being of man.

Now take the human physical body as you have it before you, take all that this physical body is as instrument of the thinking ego. You will best realize what is meant by this when you remember that the ego itself remains the same from incarnation to incarnation, but that the instrument of the ego is built up anew for each incarnation. The material tool of the ego is built up anew in each incarnation. Now man has an advantage over the whole animal kingdom in possessing a finer material organization, namely, the material organization that manifests the actual human intelligence. And this has come into existence through the fact that for long periods of time the ego has slowly and gradually learnt—although unconsciously—to work upon the astral body.

We know that man's astral body consists of two parts: one part upon which he has as yet done nothing, which is therefore as it was macrocosmically, and one part upon which he has worked. These two parts are in a certain way developed in everyone. In the higher nerve system, particularly in the brain which is built afresh with each new incarnation, you have the material expression of the work done by man's ego upon his astral body. Thus man has a much more completely developed forebrain than the animal because the front part of the brain is the manifestation of the astral body worked upon by the ego. But the astral body has nevertheless its outer expression in the nerve system as well.

Now you can easily realize that the moment some member of our organism is brought to a higher stage of perfection, an alteration must take place in the whole remaining organism. The rest of the organism must undergo a change. Why cannot a man go on four feet? Why has he transformed his front limbs to instruments of work? Because in his earthly development he has worked upon his astral body! To develop the forebrain involves perfecting the etheric instrument. The outer is always a real manifestation of the inner. All that we see in a physical state in our present phase of evolution is a result and indeed a specific result of spiritual evolution.

Now you will realize that everything material, right into the form, is a result of what stands actively behind this material. There are, for instance, beings like those I have just described to you which are unable to transform their astral body because they lack a spiritual nature. No ego works upon their astral body. This astral body with all its soul-experiences must come to expression in a material form. Yet the material form of beings through which no ego glows cannot be visible in our evolutionary phase. It cannot be visible because it lies one degree lower than our visible matter. I beg you to grasp clearly what is meant by that. If one tries to describe what constitutes a physical body, one can say that one sees it. One cannot see the etheric body because as regards substance it lies a stage higher than the physical body. Still less can one see the astral body because it lies higher still. But beneath physical matter there are also substances which cannot be seen. Of all matter only a middle strip or band is perceptible, just that strip which constitutes physical matter, perceptible to the physical eye. Just as substance continues upwards as physical foundation for the etheric and astral, so does it continue downwards and again becomes invisible. And now that we have considered the different members of the human being we shall be able to set before us the membering of these other beings.

What we call elemental beings lack an ego, but they have developed a principle below the physical body. We can say, therefore, that the principles 3, 2, 1 and minus 1 are developed in them. But there are not only beings which begin at the third principle. We have also those which begin at 2 and then have minus 1 and minus 2. And then we have still others whose highest principle is the same as man's lowest. They have developed 1, minus 1, minus 2 and minus 3. If they have a physical body it must be an invisible one. We can also say that if man's higher members were not there his physical body would look very different. When he dies the physical body is alone and disintegrates into the atoms of nature. That it is as we know it today is because it is interpenetrated by etheric body, astral body, and ego. It is true that the beings which we call gnomes and goblins have a physical body, but they do not possess what in man we call the ego. The gnomes have the physical body as their highest principle, but they have three principles below the physical body. That makes their bodies far less visible than the physical body of man. The forces lying below the physical plane prevent even what is physical in them from ever being visible to the ordinary eye. If they are to have something approaching physical substance it can only come about under powerful pressure, if external physical matter presses them together. Then their corporeality is so compressed that they lie in a congested mass and develop in the gruesome way I described earlier. The process when the outer pressure is removed, when the earth is dug away, is in general one of dissolving which is accomplished with immense rapidity, far quicker than the dissolution of the human body after death. Hence they can never be seen even though they have a physical body. They have a physical body only for one who can see through the earth. As far as the principle, the force, of this body is concerned there is something in its structure and organization which resembles the human instrument of thought. Hence those persons who portray gnomes out of a certain nature-sense are not unjustified in making their heads a special characteristic. All these symbols have their true foundation in reality. These beings have a sort of automatic intelligence because it really acts automatically. It is as if you imagine your brain to be taken out. It will not then be interpenetrated by your higher members, and as soon as it is taken out it no longer acts with higher intelligence. In this way we have before us the beings that we call gnomes. We shall then be able to throw further light on the beings that stand below man. But first we must form an idea as to where such beings stand in the course of evolution. This question is in fact by far the more important one, and is connected not only with our past evolution, but also with that in the future. That is the essential thing. And how are they connected with our future evolution?

To answer this we must consider the development of man. We know that man passes from embodiment to embodiment, from incarnation to incarnation; we know that to each new incarnation he brings with him the fruits of the previous one. We know that man himself is actually a co-creator in each new incarnation of his form as well as of his abilities and destiny. What meets him as his destiny are the deeds which he himself formerly engraved into the external world. They come back again as his destiny. What he has engraved into himself through his life comes back to him as his talents and faculties. Thus man shares in creating both —his external destiny and his inner organization.

We now ask ourselves: Where does this come from? What is it that causes us to be, let us say, at a more perfect stage of development—and every single person is at a more perfect stage in this respect? What makes us advance to a higher stage? It is all that we have taken in throughout our incarnations. We do not see through our eyes and hear through our ears to no purpose; after death we assimilate the fruits of a life and bring with us what can be effective, that from which we can build the germinal force of the next incarnation.

Now various things can occur. The little pointer of the balance can swing out towards the one or the other side. The ideal condition would be that a man in each incarnation made a thorough use of his life, that he left unused nothing which he could go through and experience and which could bear fruit for the following incarnation, but that he took everything with him. This as a rule never happens. A man oversteps either to the one side or to the other. He either uses his organization insufficiently, certain forces remain unused and he brings less into the new incarnation than he could have done, or he penetrates too deeply into his organization and becomes too closely involved in his bodily nature. There are two sorts of people. The one kind would like to live entirely in the spirit and not descend to their corporeal nature; they are called dreamers and visionaries by ordinary every-day people. The other kind descend too deeply into the body. They do not draw out from the incarnation what should be drawn out, but grow together with the incarnation. They find it sympathetic and pleasant to be with the incarnation, they do not keep for themselves what progresses from incarnation to incarnation but let it

133

sink down into what ought only to be the instrument for the eternal germ of man's being.

I pointed once before to an important legend that sets before us what a man must experience who descends too deeply into the temporary, transitory nature of the one incarnation. If we think of an extreme case, we can imagine it like this: "What is it to me that I should carry over something to later incarnations? I live in this incarnation, I like it, it suits me very well. I am not concerned further with what I am supposed to make from it." If this thought is followed out, where does it lead? It leads to a man who sits at the wayside when a great Leader of humanity passes by. He however rejects the ideas of the Leader of mankind. He repulses him and thinks: "I will know nothing of thee, who wouldst guide the kernel of my being into future incarnations where mankind will be outwardly more perfect. I wish to be united with my present form." A man who thrusts from him such a Leader of mankind will appear again in the same form. And if this attitude hardens, then he will also thrust from him the Leader in the next incarnation. He will appear again and again as the same figure.

We shall now picture those who listen to the great Leader of humanity. They will preserve the soul with its eternal life-kernel. Mankind will have gone forward but they too will appear in an ever progressed form. He however who thrusts the Leader of humanity from him must reappear again and again in the same way. That is the legend of Ahasuerus, who has thrust from him the Christ, the Leader of humanity. Man has either hardened or possesses the possibility of developing to higher stages. Races would not stay behind and become decadent if there were not men who wish to stay behind and are obliged to stay behind, since they have not developed their eternal life-kernel.

Older races only persist because there are men who cannot or will not move forward to a higher racial form. I cannot today speak about the whole series of possibilities, in the course of earthly evolution, for man to become one with the race, to grow together with what is the character of one race or another. Think of the Atlantean race; souls have gone through it, but not all have passed out of it. There are sixteen possibilities of becoming merged with the race. They are called the "sixteen paths of perdition." On these paths man would merge with the material. By striving forward, however, he is drawn up from race to race to ever higher stages.

We see then that it is actually possible for a man to combine with the one incarnation in such a way that he remains behind in evolution. His other soul-brothers are therefore at a higher stage when he reappears in a new incarnation. He must then content himself with an inferior incarnation which has been left to him in a decadent race. This is something that positively takes place. It need not frighten people, however, for the present phase of evolution. No one is obliged to take all the sixteen paths and thereby fall out of evolution. We must only be aware of the possibility.

Now let us take an extreme case and imagine that a man unites too fully with what is to constitute the character of an incarnation. Let us suppose he reaches what is to be reached in sixteen incarnations; he takes the sixteen false paths. The earth does not wait for him, the earth goes forward and he finally arrives at a point where he can no longer incorporate in a human body, for none are in existence. There will be no more bodies in which souls that have grown too much involved in their bodily nature can incarnate. Such souls lose the possibility of incarnation and find no other opportunity. Just think what they will have lost. It is possible, but only in exceptional cases, that even during Earth evolution souls will be unable to incarnate because there are no more bodies bad enough. These men have gone so far that they have no other opportunity of incarnating in the normal course of evolution. Let us suppose such beings should remain on the earth—it will only be single cases. And now, since the later is the fruit 'of the earlier, these would then find no bodies suitable for them. They are, as it were, too good for the bodies of a subordinate order and for the other bodies they are too bad. They must therefore live a bodiless 'existence. They must cut themselves off entirely from the progress of evolution. Why have they deserved this? By reason of the fact that they have not made 'use of life! The world is around them; they have possessed senses in order to perceive the world, to enrich the life-kernel and mold it to a higher stage. They do not advance with world evolution, they remain behind at a certain stage. Beings that stay behind at such stages appear in a later epoch with approximately the character of the earlier age. They have grown together with it, but not in the forms of the later epoch. They appear in a later epoch as subordinate nature-spirits. In fact the human race will furnish a whole number of such new nature-spirits in the second half of the Jupiter evolution, for man will have fully completed the fifth principle at the Jupiter stage. For those who have not used the opportunity on Earth to develop the fifth principle there will be no available form. They will appear as nature-spirits and they will appear then with four principles, the fourth being the highest. Whereas the normally advanced man will have the principles 5, 4, 3, 2 at the Jupiter stage, these men will have 4, 3, 2, 1. That would be the destiny of those who have not gradually developed their higher principles by making use of earthly life. They become nature-spirits, so to speak, of future evolutionary periods, working invisibly. Just the same occurred in the case of our present nature-spirits in the earlier periods of evolution, except in so far as there are, of course, continual changes according to the character of the different periods. Everything has now been graded, so to speak, according to moral responsibility, and because this is so, the nature-spirits that arise from the human race will have a certain morality. Upon Jupiter there will be nature-spirits which have moral responsibility.

Let us now recollect what I have said as to how Jupiter differs from our Earth. We have described the nature of the Earth as that of the planet of Love, in contrast to the nature of the Moon, the planet of Wisdom. As love has evolved on Earth so did the wisdom that we find all around us evolve on the Moon. Love in its lowest form originated in the ancient Lemurian age and becomes transformed to ever higher stages up to the highest spiritual form. When in the future the Earth planet appears as Jupiter, the Jupiter dwellers will direct their gaze upon love as men on Earth do upon wisdom. We observe the thigh bone into which wisdom is woven; the whole Earth is in a certain sense crystallized wisdom, which was formed little by little on the Moon. But wisdom was formed gradually just as on our Earth love is gradually formed. And just as we wonder at the wisdom in all that surrounds us, so he who will one day inhabit Jupiter will feel wafting towards him the love that will lie in all things. This love will stream forth from all beings and speak to us, as the wisdom speaks to us which is secreted into the Earth through the old Moon existence.

Thus the cosmos moves forward from stage to stage. The Earth is the cosmos of Love, and every condition has its special task. As a common wisdom prevails throughout our Earth, so will a common love prevail throughout Jupiter.

And as the destructive forces of wisdom originate from those beings who stayed behind on the Moon, so there will appear upon Jupiter the destructive forces of love from beings who have remained behind. Into the midst of the general tapestry of the Jupiter existence will be set the hideous forms of the retarded beings with egoistic demands for love and they will be the mighty devastating powers in the Jupiter existence. The staying behind of human beings in individual incarnations creates the destructive nature-powers on Jupiter. Thus we see how the world is woven, harmful elements as well as beneficent; we have a moral element woven into the world process.

The following table shows all the forms of nature spirits:

	Physical body & above	Below
Gnomes	1	3
Undines	2	2
Sylphs	3	1
Salamanders	4	0

Thus the Gnomes have 3 principles below and 1 above, the Undines have 2 principles below and 2 above, the Sylphs have 1 below and 3 above. They are all retarded beings which surge through the figure and form of the earth as elemental beings. They have not been able to attain to a spirit; they consist purely of body and soul. Gnomes, Undines and Sylphs are two-membered beings.

Now you will ask me where the Salamanders really come from. They are actually a fourth kind. If you ask—I can only indicate this in conclusion—whence come these three kinds, Gnomes, Sylphs, Undines, I can only answer that they are beings which have remained behind. But the Salamanders in a certain way are human, since they have partially developed the fourth principle. They are not advanced enough, however, to be able to assume human shape. Where does this fourth species come from? I will explain this in conclusion. When you understand this you will be able to understand many of the secrets of surrounding nature. You know that when we trace man back in his evolution we come to more and more spiritual forms. Man has progressed little by little to physical existence. We know that the different animal species have been gradually ejected, so to speak, as the retarded brethren of the advancing human evolution. Man attained such advanced development by being the last of all to take a physical form. The other animal creatures are at a backward stage because they were not able to wait, because they pressed into the earthly organs and physical organization earlier. But the animals have group souls which work into the physical world though they exist only on the astral plane. We see the wisdom given by the Moon to our evolution most comprehensively developed in the animal kingdom by the group souls. Man creates his civilization *through wisdom,* but he must not ascribe wisdom to himself. Any human wisdom is not merely in man, but is present in a far more comprehensive way in our whole earth planet. One who sets great store by mankind may say: "What strides humanity has made in wisdom! The recent inventions for instance are a witness to it." And now think of your school days and the principal discoveries that were told us then. Perhaps you will also remember the discovery of paper. Human wisdom got to the stage of inventing paper. It was certainly an achievement of human wisdom.

But the wasp knew it much earlier still! You all know wasps' nests. They are made of the same substance as the paper made by man. We could go through all nature and we should find ruling wisdom everywhere. How much earlier

139

than man the wasp spirit discovered paper! The individual wasp does not do it, it is the group ego.

So we see that what constitutes human wisdom is interwoven and impressed into the whole earth. But the relation of the animal to its group soul is only up to a certain point what it actually ought to be from the cosmic standpoint—if I may say so. What is this relation of the group soul to the single animal? Take perhaps the group soul of an insect species. When the single insect dies it is exactly the same for the group soul as when you lose a hair and another grows. The animal forms that come into being are only fresh creations of the group soul. You can follow up the animal ranks for a long way and everywhere you will find that what is on the physical plane has just the same action as a cloud dissolving and reforming. The group spirit is metamorphosed and its physical members merely renew themselves. That happens however only up to a certain stage, after which something else takes place in the animal kingdom. This is very important just when you come to the so called higher animals. Precisely there something occurs which no longer seems quite to fit in with what I have been describing.

Let us take as a marked case the apes. The ape, for instance, brings too much from the group soul down into its own individual existence. Whereas in the relatively lower animal the whole physical form goes back into the group soul, the ape keeps something in the physical organization which cannot go back. What the ape detaches from the group spirit can no longer return. So too in the case of man, you have the ego which goes from incarnation to incarnation and is capable through development of reaching our different stages. Here too there is no possibility of returning into the group spirit. The ape has something which is similar to the human ego.

A whole series of animals draws too much out of the group soul, others again draw something out in another way. And this remains in our evolution and works as the fourth class of elemental spirits. They are detached group souls of animals whose individual souls cannot return into the group soul, because they have carried their development beyond the normal point. From countless animals such ego-like beings remain behind. They are called Salamanders. That is the highest form, for they are ego-like.

With these remarks I have introduced you to the nature of a series of beings which we shall learn to know more exactly, for today we have only learnt their kind of existence and connections. But they work in a certain way in our world. The classification can in fact give but little; in course of time, however, we shall come as well to their description. These salamander-like beings come about even today in a strange manner, when certain human natures of specially low order, who nevertheless will certainly incarnate again, leave behind a part of their lower nature. There are such men. No human being, today, of course, can be so evil that he falls completely out of evolution, but he can leave part of his nature behind. These are then especially harmful elements within our evolution—these partially detached human natures which have remained as a species of spirit and permeate our existence. Much of what interpenetrates our spiritual space and of which we have not the least idea shows itself only too well in external phenomena. Many bad things in civilization which today seem natural will only be explained when men know with what disturbing, retarding forces they have to do. The effects will be evident in many decadent phenomena of our civilization. It is only because this is foreseen by those who know how to read the signs of the time, that the Anthroposophical Movement has been called into existence. One who stands in the world without knowledge has to let things work upon him. One who has insight, however, will be in a position to keep man free from the disturbing influences of these beings.

If you ponder this in the right way the deep spirituality and healing nature of the Anthroposophical Movement will be seen. Its aim is to free man from the forces that want to hold him back. We should fall completely into decadence if we were unwilling to concern ourselves with knowledge of these things. You will experience all sorts of crass cultural phenomena in the near future. You will find that those standing within them will look upon those people as dreamers who call things by their right names. The world has reached the pitch where those who know reality are called dreamers and visionaries, whereas the real visionaries are those who wish to cling only to the external. The progress of civilization rests upon man's penetrating with knowledge into the character of the hostile powers. Knowledge, when understood in the sense often expressed here, is something that will bring from the anthroposophical spiritual stream a certain saying to true realization. It is the saying which we have learnt in Christian esotericism, and which the Leader of Christian life proclaimed to his followers: "Ye shall know the truth and the truth shall make you free." Knowledge of full and complete truth and reality can make man free and wholly and entirely human.

IX

W E VENTURED on rather unusual ground in our last lecture when we turned our attention to certain beings who definitely exist amongst us. They are spiritual beings who in a certain way fall out of the regular course of evolution, and it is just this fact that gives them their significance. We were considering the elemental beings whose existence is naturally viewed by the enlightened mind of today as the utmost superstition, but who will play a significant rôle in a not very far distant time of our spiritual evolution, precisely through the position they occupy in the cosmos. We have seen how such elemental beings come into existence as a sort of irregularly severed parts of group souls. We need only remember what was said at the end of the lecture and we shall have placed the nature of such elemental creatures before our spiritual eyes. We were considering one of the last formed species of these elementary beings. We pointed to the fact that each animal form—or to put it differently— a totality of similarly formed animals is represented by a group soul. We have said that these group souls play the same rôle in the astral world as our human soul—in so far as it is I-endowed—in the physical world. The human ego is really a group ego which has descended from the astral plane to the physical plane, and thus becomes an individual ego. The animal egos are still normally on the astral plane, and what is here on the physical plane as the separate ani-

143

mal possesses only physical body, etheric body, and astral body. The ego is in the astral world, similarly formed animals being members of their group ego. We can realize from this fact how birth and death in human life have not the same significance in the life of the animal. For when an individual animal dies, the group soul or group ego remains alive. It is just the same as if—assuming that it were possible—a man lost a hand and was capable of replacing it. His ego would not say: 'I have died through the loss of my hand'; it would feel that it had renewed a limb. So the group ego of the lions renews a limb when a lion dies and is replaced by another. Thus we can understand that birth and death have not at all the significance for the animal group souls as they have for the human being of the present cycle of evolution. The group soul of the animals knows changes, metamorphoses; knows, so to speak, the severing of the members which then extend into the physical world, the loss of these members and their renewal.

We have said, however, that there are certain animal forms which go too far in the process of severing, which are no longer in a position to send back to the astral plane what they bring down to the physical plane. When an animal dies what falls away must be entirely exhausted in the surrounding world, while the soul and spirit nature of the animal must stream back into the group soul, to be extended afresh and grow to a new individual entity. There are in fact certain animal forms which cannot send everything back into the group soul; and these parts which remain over, which are cut loose, torn loose from the group soul, then lead an isolated life as elemental beings. Our evolution has gone through the most varied stages and at each stage such elemental beings have been separated off, so you can well imagine that we have a fairly large number of such elementals around us in what we call the supersensible world.

When, for instance, the enlightened person says that people talk of elemental beings and call them Sylphs, Lemures, but that such things do not exist—then you must reply that he does not see these things because he has not troubled to develop the organs of cognition which would enable him to recognize them. But just ask the bees, or rather, the soul of the beehive. They could not close themselves to the existence of Sylphs or Lemures! For the elemental beings which are denoted by these names are to be found at quite definite places, namely, where there is a certain contact of the animal kingdom with the plant kingdom. This has not a general application, however; they are to be found only at spots where the contact takes place under certain circumstances. When the ox eats grass there is a contact between the animal kingdom and the plant kingdom, but that is a commonplace, normal proceeding; it lies in the regular course of evolution. The contact that occurs between the bee and the blossom stands on quite a different page of cosmic evolution. Bees and blossoms are much farther apart in organization and they come together again in a special way— moreover a quite remarkable force is unfolded in their contact. The peculiar auric sheath which always arises when a bee or similar insect sucks at a flower belongs to the "interesting" observations of the spiritual-supersensible worlds —if one may use the expression, but we have so few appropriate expressions for these subtle things. The peculiar, unique experience which the little bee has when it sucks at the flower is present not only in the masticators or in the bee's body, but the exchange of taste between bee and blossom spreads out a sort of tiny etheric aura. Every time that the bee sucks there is this aura, and always when something like this arises in the supersensible world the beings which need it arrive at the spot. They are attracted by it, for there they find their food—to express it crudely again.

I said on another occasion that we should not be concerned with the question: Whence come all the beings of which we have spoken? Wherever the opportunity is given for definite beings, then they are always there. If a person sends out wrong, evil feelings, these live around him and attract beings which are there waiting, just as some physical being waits for food. I once compared this with the fact that there are no flies in a clean room; if there are all sorts of food-remains in the room, then there are flies. So it is with the supersensible beings: one need only provide them with the means of nourishment. The bee which sucks at the blossom spreads a little etheric aura and then such beings approach, especially when a whole swarm of bees settles on a tree and then moves away with the sensation of taste in the body. Then the whole swarm is ensheathed in this etheric aura and also entirely interpenetrated by the spiritual beings which one calls Sylphs or Lemures. In border-regions where different kingdoms come in touch with one another these beings are present and they really play a rôle. In fact they are not only to be found where this fine etheric aura arises, they not only approach to satisfy themselves, but they are hungry and they bring the hunger to expression by guiding the particular creatures to the particular places. In a certain way they are little guides.

So we see that beings who, we may say, have severed their connection with other worlds to which they were formerly united, have taken in exchange a strange rôle. They are beings which can well be used in other worlds. At any rate, when they are so used a kind of organization is established, they come under higher beings.

146

It was said at the beginning of today's lecture that at a by no means very distant time it will be fully necessary for humanity to know of these things. In a not very distant future, science will take an extraordinary course. Science will become increasingly materialistic, will confine itself simply to a description of external facts of the physical senses. Science will confine itself to the crudely material, although a strange transitional state still prevails today. A time of sheer undiluted materialism in science lies not very far behind us. This crude materialism is at the most still seen as a possibility by people of a purely amateur outlook, though few thinkers trouble to set something else in its place. We see a whole number of abstract theories appear in which a timid reference is made to the supersensible, the superbodily. The course of events, however, and the power of external physical facts will utterly overthrow these strange, fantastic theories which are set up by those who are dissatisfied today with physical science. And one day the learned will find themselves in a peculiar situation as regards these theories. All that they have spun out about All-Being and All-Ensouledness of this or that world, all their speculations will be overthrown and men will have nothing more in the hand than sheer sense-perceptible facts in the fields of geology, biology, astronomy, and so forth. The theories set up today will be very short-lived, and to the one who is able to look into the special course of science, an absolute desolation of the purely physical horizon is presented.

Then, however, the time will also have come when a fairly great number of representatives of humanity will be ripe to acknowledge the supersensible worlds of which the spiritual-science world-conception speaks today. Such a phenomenon as that of the bee-life in connection with what can be known of the supersensible worlds offers a wonderful answer to the great riddle of existence. These things are of great importance from yet another side. It will become increasingly indispensable to grasp the nature of the group souls, and such knowledge will play a great rôle even in the purely external evolution of humanity. If we go back thousands and thousands of years we find man himself as a being still belonging to a group soul. Human evolution on our Earth is from the group soul nature to the individual soul. Man advances through the gradual descent of his ego-endowed soul into physical conditions, there having the opportunity of becoming individual. We can observe different stages in the evolution of mankind and see how the group soul gradually becomes individual.

Let us go back to the time of the first third of the Atlantean culture epoch. There the life of man was quite different; in the bodies in which we were incorporated at that time our souls had quite different experiences. There is one experience which plays a rôle in man's life today—whether as individual or member of social group—that has undergone a great change since that time, namely, the alternation of waking and sleeping.

In ancient Atlantean times you would not have experienced the same alternation of waking and sleeping as exists today. What is then the characteristic difference in comparison with present humanity?

When the physical and etheric bodies lie in bed, the astral body with the ego lifts itself out and what one calls the modern consciousness sinks into an indefinite darkness. In the morning when the astral body and the ego draw again into the other members they make use of the physical organs and consciousness lights up. This condition of daily waking in consciousness, nightly sleeping in unconsciousness, did not exist formerly. When it was daytime and man dipped down into his physical body, as far as was the case then, he by no means saw physical beings and objects in definite boundaries as he does today. He saw everything with vague outlines just as you do when you go along the streets on a foggy evening and see the lamps surrounded with a misty aura. That was the way the human being of that time saw everything.

If that was the day condition, what was the night condition? When the human being passed out of the physical and etheric bodies during the night, no absolute unconsciousness came over him, it was only a different kind of consciousness. At that time man was still aware of the spiritual processes and spiritual beings around him, not clearly and exactly as in true clairvoyance, but with a last relic of ancient clairvoyant sight. Man lived by day in a world of hazy, nebulous outlines, in the night he lived among spiritual beings who were around him as we have the various objects around us today. There was thus no sharp division between day and night, and what is contained in saga and myths is not some folk-fantasy but memories of the experiences which early man had in the supersensible world in his then state of consciousness. Wotan or Zeus or other supersensible spiritual divinities who were known to various peoples are not fabrications of fantasy as is asserted at the council-board of erudition. Such assertions can only be made by someone who knows nothing of the nature of folk-fantasy. It does not in the least occur to early peoples to personify in that way. Those were experiences in ancient times. Wotan and Thor were beings with whom man went about as today he goes about with his fellow-men, and myths and sagas are memories of the ages of ancient clairvoyance.

We must be clear, however, that something else was united with this living into the spiritual supersensible worlds. In these worlds man felt himself not as an individual being but as a sort of limb of spiritual beings. He belonged to higher spiritual beings as our hands belong to us. The faint feeling of individuality which man possessed at that time he acquired when he dipped down into his physical body and emancipated himself from the "dance" of the divine spiritual beings. That was the beginning of his feeling of individuality. At that time man was absolutely clear about his group soul, he felt himself immersed in the group soul when he left his physical body and entered the supersensible consciousness. That was an ancient time when the human being had a vivid consciousness of belonging to a group soul, a group ego.

Let us look at a second stage of human evolution—we will omit intermediate stages—, the stage referred to in the history of the Patriarchs of the Old Testament. What really underlies this we have already related. We have given the reason why the Patriarchs Adam, Noah, and so on, had such a long life time. It was because the memory of early mankind was quite different from that of contemporary man. The memory of modern man has in fact become individual, too. He remembers what he has experienced since birth—many actually from a much later point of time. This was not the case in ancient times. At that time what the father had experienced between birth and death, what had been experienced by the grandfather, the great-grandfather, were as much an object of memory as a man's own experiences. Strange as it seems to the modern man there was a time when memory went beyond the individual and back through the whole blood relationship. The external sign for the existence of such a memory is precisely such names as Noah, Adam, and so on. These names do not denote single individuals between birth and death. Today a name is given to the one individual whose memory is enclosed between birth and death. Formerly the giving of a name went as far as the memory reached back into the generations, as far as the blood flowed through the generations.

"Adam" is merely a name that lasted as long as the memory lasted. One who does not know that the giving of names in former times was quite different from what it is today will not be able to understand the nature of these things at all. A fundamental consciousness mediating quite differently existed in ancient times. Imagine that the ancestor had had two children, each of these two again, the next generation again two, and so forth. In all of them the memory reached up to the ancestor and they felt themselves *one* in the memory which meets up above, so to speak, in a common point. The people of the Old Testament expressed this by saying—and this applies to each single adherent of the Old Testament—"I and Father Abraham are one." Each individual felt himself hidden in the consciousness of the group-soul, in the "Father Abraham."

The consciousness with which the Christ has endowed mankind surpasses that. The ego through its consciousness is connected directly with the spiritual world, and this comes to expression in: "Before Abraham was, was the I —or the I am." Here the impulse to stimulate the "I am" comes fully into the separate individual.

So we see a second stage of the evolution of mankind: the group-soul age which finds its external expression in the blood relationship of the generations. A people which has particularly developed this lays very special value on continually emphasizing: As folk we have a folk-group-soul in common.—That was particularly the case for the people of the Old Testament, and the conservatives among them strongly opposed therefore the emphasis of the "I am" of the individual ego. Whoever reads St. John's Gospel can grasp with spiritual hands, so to speak, that that is true. One need only read the story of the conversation of Jesus with the woman of Samaria at the well. Here it is expressly pointed out that Christ Jesus goes to those also who are not related by blood. Read how remarkably it is indicated: "For the Jews had no dealings with the Samaritans." One who can experience this gradually, meditatively, will see how humanity has advanced from the group soul to the individual soul.

History has become an entirely external matter, very much a "fable convenue," for it is written from documents. Suppose that something had to be written today from documents and the most important documents are lost! Then whatever documents are accidentally available are thrown together and reports are made. For matters of spiritual reality one needs no documents; they are inscribed in the Akashic Record which is a faithful record and effaces nothing. It is difficult, however, to read in the Akashic Record because the external documents are even a hindrance to the reader of spiritual "scripts." But we can see how the advance from group soul to individual soul has taken place in times lying very near to our own.

One who observes history from a spiritual aspect will have to recognize a most important period of time in the early Middle Ages. Previously man was still enclosed in various groups if only externally. To a much greater extent than is dreamt of by modern man, people at the beginning of the Middle Ages still received their significance and value even as regards their work, from relationship and other connections. It was a natural consequence for the son to do what the father did. Then came the time of the great inventions and discoveries. The world began to demand more from the purely personal proficiency, and man was increasingly torn out of the old connections. We can see the expression of this throughout the Middle Ages when cities of the same type were founded over the whole of Europe. We can still distinguish today the cities built on this type from those built on other foundations.

In the middle of the Middle Ages there was again an advance from the group soul to the individual soul. If we look into the future we must say: More and more man emancipates himself from the old group soul element and individualizes himself. If you could look back to earlier phases of man's evolution you would see how those cultures were cast in the same mold—as, for instance, Egypt and Rome. This is only in a very slight degree true of today. Humanity has now descended to the point where not only manners and customs are individual but even opinions and faiths as well. There are people among us already who look on it as a lofty ideal for everyone to have his own religion. The idea floats before quite a number that a time must come when there are as many religions and truths as persons.

This will not be the course of human evolution. It would take this course if men were to continue to follow the impulse coming today from materialism. That would lead to disharmony, to the splitting of humanity into separate individuals. Mankind, however, will only *not* take this course if such a spiritual movement as Spiritual Science is accepted. What will enter then? The great truth, the great law, will be realized that the most individual truths, those that are found in the most inward way, are at the same time those that hold good for all.

I have already commented on the fact that today there

is really general agreement upon the truths of mathematics alone, for these are the most trivial of all. No one can say that he finds mathematical truths through external experience; we find them through inwardly realizing them. If one wants to show that the three angles of a triangle make 180°, then one draws a line through the apex which is parallel to the base and lays the three angles together fan-wise; then angle a = d, b = e, c = itself, and so the three angles are equal to a straight line, that is, 180°. Anyone who has once grasped this knows that it must be so, once and for all, just as one knows that 3 × 3 = 9 after it has once been grasped. I do not think one would expect to discover that by induction.

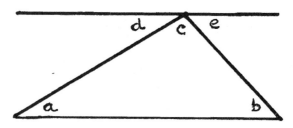

These most trivial of all truths, the arithmetical, geometrical, are found inwardly, and yet people do not dispute about them. They are in absolute agreement about them because man is far enough advanced to grasp them. Agreement of opinion prevails only as long as pure truth is not clouded by passions, sympathy and antipathy. A time will come, though it is still far distant, when mankind will be laid hold of increasingly by the knowledge of the inner world of truth. Then in spite of all individualism, in spite of truth being found by everyone for himself inwardly, harmony will prevail. If mathematical truths were not so simple and obvious then the passions aroused in acknowledging them would lead to many difficulties. For if covetousness entered in then perhaps many housewives would determine that $2 \times 2 = 5$ and not 4. These things are only so obvious and simple that they can no longer be clouded by sympathy and antipathy. Continually wider regions will be grasped by this form of truth and more peace can come to mankind if truth is grasped in this manner. The human being has grown out of the group soul condition and emancipates himself from it increasingly. If we look at groups instead of the souls, we have family connections, connections of tribe and nation, and finally connected races. The race corresponds to a group soul. All these group connections of early humanity are what man outgrows and the more we advance the more the race conception loses its meaning.

We stand today at a transitional point; race will gradually disappear entirely and something else will take its place. Those who will again grasp spiritual truth as it has been described will be led together of their own free will. Those will be the connections of a later age. The human beings of earlier times were born into connections, born into the tribe, the race. Later we shall live in the connections and associations which men create for themselves, uniting in groups with those of similar ideas while retaining their complete freedom and individuality. To realize this is necessary for a right understanding of something like the Anthroposophical Society. The Anthroposophical Society is intended to be a first example of such a voluntary association, although we may be well aware that it has not yet reached very far. The attempt had to be made to create a group in which men find themselves together without the differentiation of the ancient group soul's nature and there will be many such associations in the future. Then we shall no longer have to

155

speak of racial connections but of intellectual-ethical-moral aspects with regard to the associations that are formed.

The individuals voluntarily allow their feelings to stream together and this again causes the forming of something which goes beyond the merely emancipated man. An emancipated human being possesses his individual soul which is never lost when it has once been attained. But when men find themselves together in voluntary associations they group themselves round centres. The feelings streaming in this way to a centre once more give beings the opportunity of working as a kind of group soul, though in quite a different sense from the early group souls. All the earlier group souls were beings who made man unfree. These new beings, however, are compatible with man's complete freedom and individuality. Indeed, in a certain respect we may say that they support their existence on human harmony; it will lie in the souls of men themselves whether or not they give as many as possible of such higher souls the opportunity of descending to man. The more that men are divided, the fewer lofty souls will descend into the human sphere. The more that associations are formed where feelings of fellowship are developed with complete freedom, the more lofty beings will descend and the more rapidly the earthly planet will be spiritualized.

So we see that if man is to acquire any idea of future evolution, he must have a thorough understanding of the character of the group soul element. For otherwise, if his individual soul keeps itself aloof too long on the earth, and does not find the link of companionship, it could come about that it lets the chance of union go by. It would then itself become a sort of elemental being, and the elemental beings originating from man would be of quite an evil nature. Whereas those which have arisen from the earlier kingdoms are very useful for our orderly course of nature, the human elemental beings will by no means possess this quality.

We have seen that such severed beings arise in certain border regions, and they arise also on the boundary made by the transition from the group soul nature to the independent group associations where the connections are of an aesthetic, moral, intellectual character. Wherever such connections arise, group beings are there.

If you could observe certain spots, as, for instance, springs where underneath there is stone overgrown with moss, thus forming a kind of partition between plant and stone, and then water trickles over it—that too is essential —then you would see that what are called Nymphs and Undines are very real, an actuality. Again, where metals come in contact with the rest of the earthy realm there lie whole bundles of the beings we call Gnomes. A fourth species are the Salamanders which form, so to say, the youngest generation in the ranks of elemental beings. They nevertheless exist in large numbers. To a great extent they owe their existence to a process of separating off from animal group souls. These beings too seek opportunities for finding nourishment, and they find it in particular where not quite normal relations sometimes exist between the human and the animal kingdoms. Those who know something about these things are aware that elemental beings—and definitely good beings—develop through the intimate relationship of the rider and his steed. Through the warm connection of certain men with animal groups, feelings, thoughts and impulses arise which provide good nourishment for these elemental beings of a Salamander nature. That can be particularly observed in the united life of the shepherd and his flock, in the case of herdsmen in general who live in close connection with their animals. Certain Salamander-like elemental beings can find their nourishment in the feelings which develop through this intimacy between man and beast, and they remain where this food is to be found. They are quite shrewd too, full of a natural wisdom. Faculties develop in the shepherd through which these elemental beings can whisper to him what they know, and many of the recipes or prescriptions coming from such sources have originated in this way. A man among such conditions may well be surrounded as if by fine spiritual beings who furnish him with a knowledge of which our modern intellectuals have not the slightest idea. All these things are founded on good grounds and can definitely be observed through the methods which occult wisdom can perfect.

I should like to conclude by pointing to yet another phenomenon which can show you how certain things which are explained quite abstractly today have often sprung from a deep wisdom. I have already spoken of Atlantean times and how when men left their bodies in the night, they lived among the spiritual beings whom they called the Gods. These men were descending deeper into a physical corporeality; but the beings whom they revered as the Gods, that is, Zeus, Wotan, are on another path of evolution. They do not descend as far as the physical body, they do not touch the physical world. But even there we find certain transitional states. Man has come into existence through his whole soul and spirit being having hardened to his physical body. In the case of man the group souls in their entirety have come down to the physical plane, and man's physical body became an imprint of the group soul. Let us suppose a being like Zeus—who is a positive reality —has just slightly contacted the physical plane, just projected into it a very little. That is rather as if you dip a ball into water and it is wet underneath. In the same way certain beings in Atlantean times have only been grazed by the physical world. Physical eyes do not see what remains in the spiritual world as astral-etheric. Only the part which projects into the physical world is visible. From such projections arose symbolism in mythology. If Zeus has the eagle as symbol that is because his eagle-nature is the little projection where a being of the higher worlds touched the physical world. A great part of the bird world is severed portions of such evolving beings of the supersensible world. As with the ravens of Wotan and the eagle of Zeus so is it everywhere where symbolism goes back to occult facts. Much will become clearer to you if you take into account like this the nature and activity and evolution of the group souls in the most varied fields.

X

WHAT we have now been studying for some time in our Group-lectures is meant as a completion or expansion of the subjects that have occupied us during the winter. It may well be that a remark here or there seemed somewhat aphoristic, and we want by means of these studies to enlarge or round off thoughts and concepts that have been aroused in us.

In the last lecture we were particularly occupied with the presence of all sorts of spiritual beings which are to be found, so to speak, between the sense-perceptible kingdoms of nature that surround us. We saw especially how in the place where the beings of different nature-kingdoms come together, where the plant is pressed close to the stone at a spring, where ordinary stone impinges on a metal as constantly occurs under the earth, where there is a communion as between bee and blossom, how everywhere in such spots forces are developed which draw various beings, whom we have called elemental beings, into earthly existence. Moreover, in connection with these elemental beings we have been occupied with the fact of a certain cutting off, a detaching of beings from their whole connection. We have seen that the elemental beings called by spiritual science "Salamanders" have in part their origin from detached parts of animal group souls. These have, as it were, ventured too far forward into our physical world and have not been able to find their way back and unite again with the group soul, after the death and dissolution of the animal. We know that in the regular course of our life, the beings of our earth, the beings of the animal, plant, mineral kingdoms, have their "ego soul"—if one may so call it, have indeed such ego souls as man, differing only in the fact that the ego souls of other beings are in other worlds. We know that man is that being in our cycle of evolution who has an individual ego here on the physical plane—at least during his waking life. We know further that the beings which we call animals are so conditioned that—speaking loosely—similarly-formed animals have a group soul or group ego which is in the so-called astral world. Further, the beings which we call plants have a dreamless sleeping consciousness for the physical world here but they have group egos which dwell in the lower parts of the devachanic world; and, finally, the stones, the minerals, have their group egos in the higher parts of Devachan. One who moves clairvoyantly in the astral and devachanic worlds has intercourse there with the group souls of the animals, plants and minerals in the same way as here in the physical world he has intercourse during the day with other human souls or egos.

Now we must be clear that in many ways man is a very complicated being—we have often spoken of this complexity in different lectures. But he will appear more and more complicated the further we go into the connections with great cosmic facts. In order to realize that man is not quite the simple being which he may perhaps appear to a naive observation we need only remember that by night, from going to sleep to waking up, the man of the present evolutionary cycle is quite a different being from what he is by day. His physical and etheric bodies lie in bed, the ego with the astral body is lifted out of them. Let us consider both conditions, and in the first place the physical and etheric bodies. They lie there, and if we disregard the transitional state of dream, they have what we may call a sleep consciousness devoid of content, perceptions, or dreams. But the ego and the astral body outside have, in this present cycle of evolution, just the same dreamless sleep consciousness. The sleeping man, whether in the members remaining here in the physical world, or in those which are in the astral world, has the same consciousness as the plant covering of the earth. We must occupy ourselves a little with these two separated parts of the sleeping human being.

From other lectures we know that the man of the present time has arisen slowly and gradually. We know that he received the first rudiments of a physical body in the embodiment of our Earth lying in a primeval past which we call the Saturn evolution. We know that then in a second embodiment of our Earth, the Sun evolution, he received the etheric or life body, that in the third embodiment, the Moon evolution, he also received the astral body, and that in the present Earth embodiment of our planet he acquired what we call the ego. Thus the human being has evolved quite slowly and gradually. This physical body which man bears today is actually his oldest part, the part that has gone through most metamorphoses. It has undergone four changes. The first rudiment, received by man on ancient Saturn, has gone through three modifications, on the Sun, on the Moon, and finally on the Earth, and is expressed in man's present sense-organs. They were quite different organs on ancient Saturn, but their first rudiments were there while no other part of the physical body as yet existed. We can look on ancient Saturn as a single being, entirely consisting of sense-organs. On the Sun the etheric body was added, the physical body went through a change, and the

162

organs arose which we call today the glands, though at first they existed merely in their rudiments. Then on the Moon when the physical body had undergone a third transformation through the impress of the astral body, were added those organs which we know as the nerve organs. And finally on the Earth was added the present blood-system, the expression of the ego, as the nervous system is the expression of the astral body, the glandular system of the etheric body, and the senses system the physical expression of the physical body itself. We have seen in former lectures that the blood system appeared for the first time in our Earth evolution and we ask: Why does blood flow in the present form in the blood channels? What does this blood express? Blood is the expression of the ego and with this we will consider a possible misunderstanding, namely, that man actually misunderstands the present physical human body.

The human body as it is today is only one form of many. On the Moon, on the Sun, on Saturn, it was there but always different. On the Moon, for instance, there was as yet no mineral kingdom, on the Sun there was no plant world in our sense, and on Saturn no animal kingdom—there was solely the human being in his first physical rudiments. Now when we reflect on this we must be clear that the present human body is not only physical body, but physical-mineral body, and that to the laws of the physical world— hence it is the "physical body"—it has assimilated the laws and substances of the mineral kingdom, which permeate it today. On the Moon the physical human body had not yet assimilated those laws: if one had burnt it there would have been no ash, for there were no minerals in the present earthly sense. Let us remember that to be physical and to be mineral are two quite different things. The human body is physical because it is governed by the same laws as the stone; it is at the same time mineral because it has been impregnated with mineral substances. The first germ of the physical body was present on Saturn, but there were no solid bodies, no water, no gases. On Saturn there was nothing at all but a condition of warmth. The modern physicist knows of no such condition because he thinks that warmth can only appear in connection with gases, water, or solid objects. But that is an error. The physical body which today has assimilated the mineral kingdom was on ancient Saturn a nexus of physical laws. We are physical laws working in lines, in forms, what you learn to know as laws in physics. Externally the physical human being was manifested on Saturn purely as a being which lived in warmth. We must thus clearly distinguish between the mineral element and the actual physical principle of man's body. It is physical law which governs the physical body. It belongs, for example, to the physical principle that our ear has such a form, that it receives sound in quite a definite way; to the mineral nature of the ear belong the substances which are impregnated into this scaffolding of physical laws.

Now that we have become clear about this and realize particularly how the sense-organs, glands, nerves and blood are the expressions of our fourfold nature, let us turn again to the observation of the sleeping human being. When man is asleep the physical and etheric bodies lie on the bed, the astral body and the ego are outside. But now let us remember that the astral body is the principle of the nervous system and the ego that of the blood system. Thus during the night the astral body has deserted that part of the physical body of which, so to say, it is the cause—namely, the nervous system. For only when the astral body membered itself into man on the Moon could the nervous system arise. Thus the astral body callously leaves what belongs to it, what it is actually due to maintain, and in the same way the ego deserts that which it has called into life. The principles of the blood and of the astral body are outside and the sleeping physical and etheric bodies are absolutely alone. But now nothing of a material physical nature can subsist in the form which has been called forth by a spiritual principle when this spiritual principle is no longer there. That is quite out of the question. Never can a nervous system live unless astral beings are active in it, and never can a blood system live unless ego-beings are active in it. Thus you all meanly desert in the night your nervous and blood systems and relinquish them to other beings of an astral nature. Beings which are of the same nature as your ego now descend into your organism. Every night the human organism is occupied by beings fitted to maintain it. The physical body and the etheric body which lie on the bed are at the same time interpenetrated by these astral and ego beings; they are actually within the physical body. We might call them intruders, but that is in no sense correct. We ought in many ways to call them guardian spirits, for they are the sustainers of what man callously deserts in the night.

Now it is not so bad for man to leave his bodies every night. I have already said that the astral body and the ego are perpetually active in the night. They rid the physical body of the wear and tear which the day has given, which in a broad sense we call fatigue. Man is refreshed and renewed in the morning because during the night his astral body and ego have removed the fatigue which were given him by the impressions of daily life. This all-night activity of the astral body in getting rid of the fatigue substances is a definite fact to clairvoyant perception. The ego and astral body work from outside on the physical and etheric bodies. But in the present cycle of his evolution man is not yet advanced enough to be able to carry out such an activity quite independently. He can only do so under the guidance of other, higher beings. So the human being is taken every night into the bosom of higher beings, as it were, and they endow him with the power of working in the right way on his physical and etheric bodies. These at the same time are the beings—that is why we may not call them intruders—who care for man's blood and nerve systems in the right way in the night.

As long as no abnormalities arise the co-operation of spiritual beings with man is justified. But such irregularities can very well enter and here we come to a chapter of spiritual science which is extraordinarily important for the practical life of the human soul. One would like it to be known in the widest circles and not only theoretically but as giving the foundation for certain activities of the human soul life. It is not generally imagined that the facts of the soul life have a far-reaching effect. In certain connections I have also called your attention to the fact that it is only when viewed in the light of spiritual science that events in the life of the soul can find their true explanation. We all know the deep significance of the statement: "Regarded from the spiritual-scientific aspect a lie is a kind of murder." I have explained that a sort of explosion really takes place in the astral world when man utters a lie—even, in a certain way, if he only thinks it. Something takes place in the spiritual world when man lies, which has a far more devastating effect for that world than any misfortune in the physical world. But things which one relates at a certain stage of spiritual-scientific observation, characterizing them as far as is possible then, gain more and more clearness and confirmation when one advances in the knowledge of spiritual science.

Today we shall learn of another effect of lying, slandering, although these words are not used here in the ordinary crude sense. When more subtly, out of convention, for instance, or out of all sorts of social or party considerations, people color the truth, we there have to do with a lie in the sense of spiritual science. In many respects man's whole life is saturated, if not with lies, yet with manifestations bearing an untruthful coloring. The enlightened materialist can at any rate see that an impression is made on his physical body if he receives a blow on the skull from an axe, or if his head is cut off by the railway, or he has an ulcer somewhere or is attacked by bacilli. He will then admit that effects are produced on the physical body. What is not usually considered at all is that man is a spiritual unity, that what happens in his higher members, the astral body and ego, has positive effect right down into his physical nature. It is not considered, for instance, that the uttering of lies and untruthfulness, untruth even in the affairs of life, has a definite effect on the human physical body. Spiritual vision can experience the following: If a person, let us say, has told a lie during the day, its effect remains in the physical body and is to be seen by clairvoyant perception while the person sleeps. Let us suppose this person is altogether untruthful, piling up lies, then he will have many such effects in his physical body. All this hardens, as it were, in the night, and then something very important happens. These hardenings, these "enclosures," in the physical body are not at all agreeable to the beings who from higher worlds must take possession of the physical body in the night and carry out the functions otherwise exercised by the astral body and ego. The result is that in the course of life and by reason of a body diseased—one might say—through lies, portions of those beings who descend into man at night become detached. Here we have again detachment processes and they lead to the fact that when a man dies his physical body does not merely follow the paths which it would normally take. Certain beings are left behind, beings which have been created in the physical body through the effect of lying and slander, and have been detached from the spiritual world. Such beings, detached in this circuitous way, now flit and whir about in our world and belong to the class that we call "phantoms." They form a certain group of elemental beings related to our physical body and invisible to physical sight. They multiply through lies and calumnies, and these in actual fact populate our earthly globe with phantoms. In this way we learn to know a new class of elemental beings.

- But now, not only lies and slanders but also other things belonging to the soul life produce an effect on the human body. It is lies and slanders which so act on the physical body that a detaching of phantoms is caused. Other things again work in a similar way on the etheric body. You must not be amazed at such phenomena of the soul: in spiritual life one must be able to take things with all calmness. Matters, for example, which have a harmful result on the etheric body are bad laws, or bad social measures prevailing in a community. All that leads to want of harmony, all that makes for bad adjustments between man and man, works in such a way through the feeling which it creates in the common life that the effect is continued into the etheric body. The accumulation in the etheric body caused through these experiences of the soul brings about again detachments from the beings working in from the spiritual worlds and these likewise are now to be found in our environment—they are "spectres" or "ghosts." Thus these beings that exist in the etheric world, the life world, we see grow out of the life of men. Many a man can go about amongst us and for one who is able to see these things spiritually, his physical body is crammed, one might say, with phantoms, his etheric body crammed with spectres, and as a rule after a man's death or shortly afterwards all this rises up and disperses and populates the world.

So we see how subtly the spiritual events of our life are continued, how lies, calumnies, bad social arrangements, deposit their creations spiritually among us on our earth. But now you can also understand that if in normal daily life the physical body, etheric body, astral body, and ego belong together, and the physical body and etheric body have to let other beings press in and act upon them, then the astral body and the ego are not in a normal condition either. At any rate they are in a somewhat different position as regards the physical and etheric bodies. These two have in sleeping man the consciousness of the plants. But the plants on the other hand have their ego above in Devachan. Hence the physical and etheric bodies of sleeping man must likewise be sustained by beings which unfold their consciousness from Devachan. Now it is true that man's astral body and ego are in a higher world, but he himself also sleeps dreamlessly like the plants. That the plants have only a physical and an etheric body and that man in his sleeping condition possesses further an astral body and ego, makes no difference as regards the plant-nature. True, man has been drawn upwards into the spiritual, the astral world, but yet not high enough upwards with his ego, to justify the sleep-condition. The consequence is that beings must now enter his astral body too when the human being goes to sleep. And so it is: influences from the devachanic world press all the time into man's astral body. They need not in the least be abnormal influences, they may come from what we call man's higher ego. For we know that man is gradually rising to the devachanic world, in as much as he approaches ever nearer to a state of spiritualization, and what is being prepared there sends its influences into him today when he sleeps. But there are not merely these normal influences. This would simply and solely be the case if human beings were fully to understand what it is to value and esteem the freedom of another. Mankind at present is still very far removed from that. Think only how the modern man for the most part wants to over-rule the mind of another, how he cannot bear someone else to think and like differently, how he wants to work upon the other's soul. In all that works from soul to soul in our world, from the giving of unjustifiable advice to all those methods which men employ in order to overwhelm others, in every act that does not allow the free soul to confront the free soul, but employs, even in the slightest degree, forcible means of convincing and persuasion, in all this, forces are working from soul to soul which again so influence these souls that it is expressed in the night in the astral body. The astral body gets those "enclosures" and thereby beings are detached from other worlds and whir through our world again as elemental beings. They belong to the class of demons. Their existence is solely due to the fact that intolerance and oppression of thought have in various ways been used in our world. That is how these hosts of demons have arisen in our world.

Thus we have learnt again today to know of beings which are just as real as the things which we perceive through our physical senses, and which very definitely produce effects in human life. Humanity would have advanced quite differently if intolerance had not created the demons which pervade our world, influencing people continually. They are at the same time spirits of prejudice. One understands the intricacies of life when one learns about these entanglements between the spiritual world in the higher sense and our human world. All these beings, as we have said, are there, and they whiz and whir through the world in which we live.

Now let us remember something else which has also been said before. We have pointed out that in the man of the last third of the Atlantean age, before the Atlantean flood, the relation of etheric body to physical body was quite different from what it had been earlier. Today the physical part of the head and the etheric part practically coincide. That was quite different in ancient Atlantis; there we have the etheric part of the head projecting far out—especially in the region of the forehead. We now have a central point for the etheric and physical parts approximately between the eyebrows. These two parts came together in the last third of the Atlantean age and today they coincide. Thereby man is able to say "I" to himself and feel an independent personality. Thus the etheric and physical bodies of the head have joined together. This has come about so that man could become the sense being that he is within our physical world, so that he can enrich his inner life through what he takes in through sense impressions, through smell, taste, sight, and so on. All of this becomes embodied in his inner being so that having obtained it he can use it for the further development of the whole cosmos. What he thus acquires can be acquired in no other way, and therefore we have always said we must not take Spiritual Science in an ascetic sense, as a flight from the physical world. All that happens here is taken with us out of the physical world

171

and it would be lost to the spiritual world if it were not collected here first.

But humanity is now getting nearer and nearer to a new condition. In this Post-Atlantean age we have gone through various culture epochs: the old Indian, the ancient Persian, lying before the time of Zarathustra, then the epoch which we have called the Babylonian-Assyrian-Chaldean-Egyptian, then the Greco-Latin, and now we stand in the fifth culture-epoch of the Post-Atlantean age. Ours will be followed by a sixth and a seventh epoch. Whereas in the course of past ages and up to our own time the united structure of our etheric and physical bodies has always grown firmer, more closely united inwardly, man is approaching a period in the future when the etheric body gradually loosens itself again and becomes independent. The way back is taken. There are people today who have a much looser etheric body than others. This loosening of the etheric body is only right for man if during his different incarnations in those culture-epochs he has absorbed so much into himself that when his etheric body goes out again it will take with it the right fruits from the physical sense world of the earth, fruits suitable for incorporation into the increasingly independent etheric body. The more spiritual are the concepts which man finds within the physical world, the more he takes with him in his etheric body. All the utilitarian ideas, all the concepts bound up with machine and industry which only serve outer needs and the outer life, and which man absorbs in our present earthly existence, are unsuitable for incorporation in the etheric body. But all the concepts he absorbs of the artistic, the beautiful, the religious—and everything can be immersed in the sphere of wisdom, art, religion—all this endows man's etheric body with the capability and possibility of being organized independently. Since this can be seen in advance, it has often been emphasized here that the world-conception of spiritual science must send its impulses and activities into practical life. Spiritual science must never remain a conversational subject for tea-parties or any other pursuit apart from ordinary life; it must work its way into the whole of our civilization. If spiritual-scientific thoughts are one day understood, then men will understand that everything our age accomplishes must be permeated by spiritual principles. Many human beings, among them Richard Wagner, foresaw in certain fields such a penetration with spiritual principles. Some day men will understand how to build a railway-station so that it streams out truth like a temple and is in fact simply an expression suited to what is within it. There is still very much to do. These impulses therefore must be effective and they will be effective when spiritual-scientific thoughts are more fully understood.

I still have a vivid recollection of a rectorial address given about twenty-five years ago by a well-known architect. He spoke about style in architecture and uttered the remarkable sentence: "Architectural styles are not invented, they grow out of the spiritual life!" At the same time he showed why our age, if indeed it produces architectural styles, only revives old ones and is incapable of finding a new style because it has as yet no inner spiritual life. When the world creates spiritual life again then all will be possible. Then we shall feel that the human soul shines towards us from all we look at, just as in the Middle Ages every lock on a door expressed what man's soul understood of outer forms. Spiritual science will not be understood till it meets us everywhere in this way as if crystallized in forms. But then mankind too will live as spirit in the spirit. Then, however, man will be preparing more and more something that he takes with him when he again rises into the spiritual world, when his etheric body becomes self-dependent. Thus must men immerse in the spiritual world if evolution is to go further in the right way.

Nothing symbolizes the permeation of the world with the spirit so beautifully as the story of the miracle of Pentecost. When you contemplate it, it is as though the interpenetration of the world with spiritual life were indicated prophetically through the descent of the "fiery tongues." Everything must be given life again through the spirit, that abstract intellectual relation which man has to the yearly festivals must also become concrete and living again. Now, at this time of Pentecost, Whitsuntide, let us try to occupy our souls with the thoughts that can proceed from today's lecture. Then the Festival, which as we know is established on a spiritual foundation, will again signify something living for man when his etheric body is ripe for spiritual creation. But if man does not absorb the Whitsuntide spirit then the etheric body goes out of the physical body and is far too weak to overcome what has already been created, those worlds of spectres, phantoms, demons, which the world creates as phenomena existing at its side.

XI

IN OUR last study evenings various aspects were brought forward which all pointed to the hidden co-operation between man and the spiritual worlds. Spiritual beings are actually around us continually, and not only around us but, in a certain respect, continually passing through us; we live with them all the time. We must not suppose, however, that a relation is established between man and the spiritual beings of his environment, merely in the somewhat cruder respect which we considered in our last studies. A relation is also formed between man and the spiritual world through his many varied interests of thought and deeds. In our last two studies we have had to indicate spiritual beings of a somewhat subordinate character. But from earlier lectures we know that we also have to do with spiritual beings who stand above man and that connections and relationships likewise exist between man and more sublime spiritual beings. We have said that there are lofty spiritual beings living around us who do not consist of physical body, etheric body, astral body, and so on, upwards, as man, but who have an etheric body as their lowest member. They are invisible to ordinary sight since their bodily nature is a fine etheric one and man's gaze looks through it. And then we come to still higher spiritual beings whose lowest member is the astral body, presenting an even less dense bodily nature.

All these beings stand in a certain relation to man, and the main point for us today is this: Man can positively so act as to come into quite definite relations to such beings here in his life on earth. According as men here on the earth do this or that in their situation in life, so do they establish all the time relationship with the higher worlds, however improbable that may seem to the man of the present enlightened age—as one says—which is not in the least enlightened in regard to many deep truths of life.

Let us take in the first place beings who have as their lowest bodily nature an etheric body, who live around us in this fine etheric body, and send down to us their forces and manifestations. Let us set such beings mentally before us and ask ourselves: Can man do something on this earthly planet—or better—have men from time immemorial done something so as to give these beings a link, a bridge, through which they come to a more intensive influence upon the whole human being? Yes, from time immemorial men have done something towards it! We must go deeper into many feelings and ideas that we touched on in the last lectures if we would form a clear thought about this bridge.

We picture then that these beings live, so to speak, out of the spiritual worlds and extend their etheric body forward from there; they need no physical body like man. But there is a physical bodily element through which they can bring their etheric body into connection with our earthly sphere—an earthly bodily element which we can set up and which forms a bond of attraction for these beings to descend with their etheric bodies and find an opportunity to dwell among men.

Such opportunities for spiritual beings to dwell among men are given, for instance, by the temple of Greek architecture, the Gothic cathedral. When we set up in our earthly sphere those forms of physical reality with the relationship of lines and forces possessed by a temple or a plastic work of sculpture, then these form an opportunity for the etheric bodies of these beings to press on all sides into these works of art which we have set up. Art is a true and actual uniting link between man and the spiritual worlds. In those forms of art expressed in space we have on earth physical bodily conditions into which beings with etheric bodies sink down.

Beings which have the astral body as their lowest member need, however, something different here on earth as the bond between the spiritual world and our earth, and that is the art of music, the phonetic art. A space through which stream musical tones is an opportunity for the freely-changing, self-determined astral body of higher beings to manifest in it. The Arts and what they are for man thus acquire a very real significance. They form the magnetic forces of attraction for the spiritual beings whose mission it is to have a connection with man, and who wish to have it. Our feelings are deepened towards human artistic creation and acquire an appreciation of art when we look at things in this way. Yet they can be deepened still more if we realize from spiritual science the true source of man's artistic creation and artistic appreciation. To come to this realization we must consider in somewhat more detail the different forms of man's consciousness.

On various occasions, as you know, we have pointed out that in the waking man the physical body, etheric body, astral body and ego are all before us, while in the sleeping man the physical and etheric bodies lie on the bed, the ego and astral body are outside them. For our present purpose it will be well to observe in more detail these two states of consciousness which alternate for everyone within twenty-four hours. In the first place man has the physical body, then the etheric or life body, then what we call roughly the astral body, the soul body, which belongs to the astral body but is united with the etheric body. That is the member which is possessed too by the animal here below on the physical plane. But then we know—and you can read it in my *Theosophy*—that united with these three members is what one generally comprises under "I." The "I" is actually a threefold being: sentient soul, intellectual or mind soul, consciousness soul, and we know that the consciousness soul is again connected with what we call spirit-self or Manas. If we place this more particularized membering of the human being before us then we can say:

What we call the sentient soul—which moreover belongs to the astral body and is of astral nature—detaches itself when man goes to sleep, but a part of the soul body remains in connection with the etheric body that lies on the bed. What is essentially withdrawn is sentient soul, intellectual or mind soul, and consciousness soul; with the waking man all this is bound together and active in him all the time. Thus whatever goes on in the physical body works on the whole inner nature, on sentient soul, intellectual soul, and also on the consciousness soul. All that works upon man in ordinary life with its disorder and chaos, the disordered impressions which he receives from morning to evening— only think of the impressions from the din and rattle of a great city—these are all continued into the members which in waking consciousness are united with the physical and etheric bodies. In the night man's inner being—sentient soul, intellectual soul, consciousness soul—is in the astral world and from there draws for itself the forces and harmonies which have been lost for it through the chaotic impressions of the day. What in a comprehensive sense we

178

call man's ego-soul is thus in a more ordered, more spiritual world than during the day. In the morning the inner soul nature emerges from this spirituality and enters the threefold bodily nature of physical body, etheric body and that part of the astral body which is united with the etheric body, even during the night.

Now if man were never to sleep, that is, were never to draw fresh strengthening forces out of the spiritual world, then everything living in his physical body and permeating it with forces would become increasingly undermined. Since, however, a strong inner nature submerges every morning into the forces of the physical body, new order enters, one might say there is a rebirth of the forces. Thus man's soul element brings with it from the spiritual world something for each of the body's members, something which works when the inner soul nature and the outer physical instrument are together.

Now what takes place in the interaction of the soul inwardness and the actual physical instrument is able—if man is sensitive in the night for the reception of the harmonies in the spiritual world—to permeate the forces—not the substances—of the physical body, with what one might call the "forces of space." Since in our present civilization man is so much estranged from the spiritual world, these "space-forces" have little effect upon him. Where the inner being of the soul clashes with the densest member of the human body, the forces have to be very strong if they are to manifest in the robust physical body. In older culture-epochs the soul brought back impulses with it that permeated the · physical body and men therefore perceived that forces were always going through physical space, that it was by no means an indifferent empty space but interwoven by forces in every direction. There was a feeling for this distribution of forces in space which was caused through the relationships that have been described. You can realize this through an example.

Think of one of the painters belonging to the great times of art when there was still a strong feeling for the forces working in space. You could see in the work of such a painter how he paints a group of three angels in space. You stand before the picture and have a definite feeling: These angels cannot fall, it is obvious that they are hovering, they support each other mutually through the active forces of space. People who make this inner dynamic their own through that interaction of the inner soul and the physical body have the feeling: That must be so, the three angels maintain themselves in space. You will find this in the case of many of the older painters, less so in more recent ones. However greatly one may esteem Böcklin, the figure which hovers above his "Pietà" produces in everyone the feeling that at any moment it must tumble down, it does not support itself in space.

All these forces going to and fro in space which are to be felt so strongly are realities, actualities—and all architecture proceeds out of this space-feeling. The origin of genuine architecture is solely the laying of stone or brick in the lines there already in space—one does nothing at all but make visible what is already present in space ideally, spiritually laid out; one fills in material. In the purest degree this feeling of space was possessed by the Greek architect who brought to manifestation in all the forms of his temple what lives in space, what one can feel there. The simple relation, that the column supports either the horizontal or the sloping masses—embodied lines, as it were—is purely a reproduction of spiritual forces to be found in space, and the whole Grecian temple is nothing else than a filling-out with material

180

of what is living in space. The Greek temple is therefore the purest architectural thought, crystallized space. And however strange it may seem to the modern man, because the Greek temple is a physical corporeality put together out of thoughts, it is the opportunity for those figures whom the Greeks have known as the figures of their Gods to come with their etheric bodies into real contact with the spatial lines familiar to them and be able to dwell within them.

It is more than a mere phrase to say that the Grecian temple is a dwelling-place of the God. To someone having a real feeling in such matters the Greek temple has a quality that makes one picture that far and wide no human being existed, nor was there anyone inside it. The Greek temple needs no-one to observe it, no-one to enter it. Think to yourself of the Greek temple standing alone and far and wide there is no-one. It is then as it should be at its most intensive. Then it is the shelter of the God who is to dwell in it, because the God can dwell in the forms. Only thus does one really understand Greek architecture, the purest architecture in the world.

Egyptian architecture—let us say, in the Pyramids—is something quite different. We can only touch on these things now. There the spatial relations, the space-lines, are so arranged that in their forms they point the paths to the soul to float up to the spiritual worlds. We are given the forms that are expressed in the Egyptian Pyramids from the paths taken by the soul from the physical world into the spiritual world. And in every kind of architecture we have thoughts that are only to be understood by spiritual cognition.

In the Romanesque architecture with its rounded arches, which has formed churches with central and side naves, with transept and apse, so that the whole is a Cross and closed above by the cupola, we have the spatial thoughts derived from the tomb. You cannot think of the Romanesque building as you think of the temple. The Greek temple is the abode of the God. The Romanesque building can only be thought of as representing a burial place. The crypt requires men in the midst of life to stand within it, yet it is a place that draws together all feelings relating to the preservation and sheltering of the dead. In the Gothic building you have again a difference. Just as it is true that the Grecian temple can be thought of with no human soul anywhere near—though it is inhabited, being the abode of the God—so is it true that the Gothic cathedral closed above by its pointed arches is not to be imagined without the congregation of the faithful within. It is not complete in itself. If it stands solitary, it is not the whole. The people within belong to it with their folded hands, folded just as the pointed arches. The whole is only there where the space is filled by the feelings of the pious faithful.

These are the forces becoming active in us and felt in the physical body as a feeling of oneself-in-space. The true artist feels space thus and molds it architecturally.

If we now pass upwards to the etheric body, we again have what the inmost soul assimilates at night in the spiritual world and brings with it when it slips again into the etheric body. What is thus expressed in the etheric body is perceived by the true sculptor and he impresses it into the living figure. That is not the space-thought but rather the tendency to show by the living form what nature has offered him. The greater understanding possessed by the Greek artist, in his Zeus, for example, has been brought with him out of the spiritual world and made alive to him when it comes in contact with the etheric body.

Further, a similar interaction takes place with what we call the soul body. When the inner soul nature meets with the soul body there arises in the same way the feeling for the first elements of painting, as the feeling for the guidance of the line. And through the fact that in the morning the sentient soul unites with the soul body and permeates it, there arises the feeling for the harmony of color.

Thus to begin with we have the three forms of art which work with external means, taking their material from the outer world.

Now since the intellectual or mind soul takes flight into the astral world every night, something else again comes about. When we use the expression "intellectual soul" in the sense of spiritual science, we must not think of the dry commonplace intellect of which we speak in ordinary life. For spiritual science "intellect" is the sense for harmony which cannot be embodied in external matter, the sense for harmony experienced inwardly. That is why we say "intellectual or mind soul." Now when this intellectual or mind soul dips every night into the harmonies of the astral world and becomes conscious of them in the astral body—though this same astral body in modern man has no consciousness of its inner nature—then the following occurs. In the night the soul has lived in what has always been called the "Harmony of the Spheres," the inner laws of the spiritual world, those Sphere Harmonies to which the ancient Pythagorean School pointed and which one who can perceive in the spiritual world understands as the relationships of the great spiritual universe. Goethe too pointed to this when he lets Faust at the beginning of the poem be transported into heaven, and says:

"The sun, with many a sister-sphere,
Still sings the rival psalm of wonder,

183

And still his fore-ordained career
Accomplishes, with tread of thunder." *

And he remains in imagery when in Part II, where Faust is
again lifted into the spiritual world, he uses the words:

"And, to spirit ears loud ringing,
Now the new-born day is springing.
Rocky portals clang asunder,
Phoebus' wheels roll forth in thunder.
What a tumult brings the light!
Loud the trump of dawn hath sounded,
Eye is dazzled, ear astounded,
The Unheard no ear may smite." *

That is to say, the soul lives during the night in these
sounds of the spheres and they are enkindled when the astral
body becomes aware of itself. In the creative musician the
perceptions of the night consciousness struggle through
during the day consciousness and become memories—memories of astral experiences, or in particular, of the intellectual
or mind soul. All that men know as the art of music is the
expressions, imprints, of what is experienced unconsciously
in the sphere harmonies, and to be musically gifted means
nothing else than to have an astral body which is sensitive
during the day condition to what whirs through it the whole
night. To be unmusical means that the condition of the astral
body does not allow of such memory arising. It is the instreaming of tones from a spiritual world which man experiences in the musical art. And since music creates in our
physical world what can only be kindled in the astral, I therefore said that it brings man in connection with those beings
who have the astral body as their lowest member. With
these beings man lives in the night; he experiences their

* Latham's translation.

184

deeds in the sphere harmonies and in the life of day expresses them through his earthly music, so that in earthly music the sphere harmonies appear like a shadow image. And in as much as the element of these spiritual beings breaks into this earthly sphere, weaves and lives through our earthly sphere, they have the opportunity of plunging their astral bodies again into the ocean waves of music, and so a bridge is built between these beings and man through art. Here we see how at such a stage what we call the art of music arises.

Now what does the consciousness soul perceive when it is immersed in the spiritual world at night—though in the present human cycle man is unconscious of it? It perceives the words of the spiritual world. It receives whispered tidings which can be received from the spiritual world alone. Words are whispered to it and when they are brought through into the day consciousness they appear as the fundamental forces of the poetic art. Thus poetry is the shadow image of what the consciousness soul experiences in the night in the spiritual world. And here let us realize in our thoughts how through man's connection with the higher worlds—and only so—in the five arts of architecture, sculpture, painting, music, poetry, he brings into existence on our earthly globe adumbrations, manifestations of spiritual reality. This is only the case, however, when art is actually lifted above mere outer sense perception. In what one today speaking broadly calls naturalism, where man merely imitates what he sees in the outer world, there is nothing of what he brings with him. The fact that we have such a purely external art in many fields today, copying only what is outside, is a proof that men in our time have lost connection with the divine spiritual world. The man whose whole interest is merged in the external physical world, in what his external senses hold alone to be of value, works so strongly on his astral bodily nature through this exclusive interest in the physical world, that this becomes blind and deaf when it is in the spiritual worlds at night. The sublimest sphere sounds may resound, the loftiest spiritual tones may whisper something to the soul, it brings nothing back with it into the life of day. And then men scoff at idealistic, at spiritual art, and maintain that art's sole purpose is to photograph outer reality, for there alone it has solid ground under its feet.

That is the way the materialist talks since he knows nothing of the realities of the spiritual world. The true artist talks differently. He perhaps will say: When the tones of the orchestra sound to me, it is as if I heard the speech of archetypal music whose tones sounded before there were yet human ears to hear them.—He can say too: In the tones of a symphony there lies a knowledge of higher worlds which is loftier and more significant than anything which can be proved by logic, analyzed in conclusions.

Richard Wagner has brought to expression both these utterances. He wanted to bring humanity to an intense feeling that where there is true art there must at the same time be elevation above the external sense element. If spiritual science says that something lives in man which goes beyond man, something superhuman that is to appear in ever greater perfection in future incarnations, so does Richard Wagner feel when he says: I want no figures striding over the stage like commonplace men in the earthly sphere.—He wants men exalted above ordinary life and so he takes mythological figures who are formed on a grander scale than normal man. He seeks the superhuman in the human. He wants to represent in art the whole human being with all the spiritual worlds as they shine upon the man of the physical earth. At a relatively early time of life two pictures stood before him—Shakespeare and Beethoven. In his artistically brilliant visions he saw Shakespeare in such a way that he said: If I gather together all that Shakespeare has given to humanity, I see there in Shakespeare figures who move over the stage and perform deeds. Deeds—and words too are deeds in this connection—happen when the soul has felt what cannot be shown externally in space, what lies already behind it. The soul has felt the whole scale from pain and suffering to joy and happiness and has experienced how from this or that nuance this or that deed is performed. In the Shakespearean drama, thinks Richard Wagner, everything appears merely in its consequences, where it acquires spatial form, where it becomes deed. That is a dramatic art which alone can display the inner nature externalized; and man can at most guess what lives in the soul, what goes on while the deed is performed.

Beside this there appeared to him the picture of the symphonist, and he saw in the symphony the reproduction of what lives in the soul in the whole emotional scale of sorrow and pain, joy and happiness in all their shades. In the symphony it comes to life—so he said to himself—but it does not become action, it does not step out into space. And he brought before his soul a picture that led him towards the feeling that once upon a time this inner nature had, as it were, broken asunder in artistic creation in order to stream outwards into the Ninth Symphony.

From these two artist-visions the idea arose in his soul of uniting Beethoven and Shakespeare. We should have to travel a long road if we would show how through his unique handling of the orchestra Richard Wagner sought to create that great harmony between Shakespeare and Beethoven so that the internal expresses itself in tone and at the same time flows into the action. Secular speech was not enough for him, since it is the means of expression for the events of the physical plane. The language that alone can be given in the tones of song became his expression of what surpasses the physically human as superhuman.

Spiritual Science does not need merely to be expressed by words, to be felt by thoughts; Spiritual Science is life. It lives in the world process, and when one says that it is to lead together the various divided currents of man's soul into one great stream, we see this feeling live in the artist who sought to combine the different means of expression so that what lives in the whole may come to expression in the one. Richard Wagner has no wish to be merely musician, merely dramatist, merely poet. All that we have seen flow down from the spiritual worlds becomes for him a means of uniting in the physical world with something still higher. He has a presentiment of what men will experience when they grow more and more familiar with that evolutionary epoch into which mankind must indeed enter, when spirit-self or Manas unites with what man has brought with him from past ages. And a divining of that great human impulse of uniting what has appeared for ages to be separated lies in Richard Wagner in the streaming together of the individual modes of artistic expression. He had a premonition of what human cultural life will be when all that the soul experiences is immersed in the principle of spirit-self or Manas, when the full nature of the soul will be immersed in the spiritual worlds. It is of profound importance when viewed as spiritual history that in art the first dawn has appeared for mankind for the approach towards the future—a future that beckons humanity, when all that man has won in various realms will flow together into an All-culture, a comprehensive culture. The arts in a certain way are the actual forerunners of a spirituality which reveals itself in the sense

188

world. Far more important than Richard Wagner's separate statements in his prose writings is the main feature that lives in them, the religious wisdom, the sacred fire which streams through all and which comes to finest expression in his brilliant essay on Beethoven, where you must read between the lines, but where you can feel the breath of air of the approaching dawn.

Thus we see how spiritual science can give a deeper view of what men bring about in their deeds. We have seen today in the field of the arts that there man accomplishes something whereby, if we may say so, the Gods may dwell with him, whereby he secures to the Gods an abode in the earthly sphere. If it is brought to man's consciousness through Spiritual Science that spirituality stands in mutual relationship with physical life—this has been done in physical life by art. And spiritual art will always permeate our culture if men will but turn their minds to true spirituality. Through such reflections the mere teaching, mere world conception of spiritual science is expanded to impulses which can penetrate our life and tell us what it ought to become and must become. For the musical-poetic art it was in Richard Wagner that the new star has first arisen which sends to earth the light of spiritual life. Such a life impulse must increasingly expand until the whole outer life becomes again a mirror of the soul.

All that meets us from without can become a mirror of the soul. Do not take that as a mere superficiality, but as something that one can acquire from spiritual science. It will be as it was centuries ago, where in every lock, in every key, we met with something that reflected what the craftsman had felt and experienced. In the same way when there is again true spiritual life in humanity, the whole of life, all that meets us outside, will appear to us again as an image of the soul. Secular buildings are only secular as long as man is incapable of imprinting the spirit into them. Spirit can be imprinted everywhere. The picture of the railway station can flash up, artistically conceived. Today we have not got it. But when it is realized again what forms ought to be, one will feel that the locomotive can be formed architecturally and that the station can be related to it as the outer envelopment of what the locomotive expresses in its architectural forms. Only when they are architecturally conceived will they be mutually related as two things belonging to each other. But then too it is not a matter of indifference how left and right are used in the forms. When man learns how the inner expresses itself in the outer, then there will be a culture again. There have indeed been ages when as yet no Romanesque, no Gothic architecture existed, when those who bore in their souls the dawn of a new culture were gathered together in the catacombs below the old Roman city. But that which lived within them and could only be engraved in meagre forms in the ancient earth-caves, that which you find on the tombs of the dead, this lit up dimly there and is what then appears to us in the Romanesque arches, the Romanesque pillars, the apse. Thought has been carried forth into the world. Had the first Christians not borne the thought in the soul it would not meet us in what has become world culture. The theosophist only feels himself as such when he is conscious that in his soul he carries a future culture. Others may ask what he has already accomplished. Then he says to himself: What did the Christians of the catacombs accomplish, and what has grown from it?

The feeble emotional impulse that lives in our souls when we sit together, let us seek to expand it in the spirit, somewhat as the thoughts of the Christians were able to expand to the vaulted wonders of the later cathedral. What we have in the hours when we are together, let us imagine expanded outwardly, carried forth into the world. Then we have the impulses which we should have when we are conscious that spiritual science is no hobby for individuals sitting together, but something that should be carried out into the world. The souls who sit here in your bodies will find, when they appear in a new incarnation, many things already realized which live in them today. Let us bring such thoughts with us when we are together. for the last time in a season and review the spiritual-scientific thoughts of the winter. Let us so transform them that they shall work as culture impulses. Let us seek in this way to steep our souls in feelings and sensations and let that live into the summer sunshine which shows us outwardly in the physical world the active cosmic forces. Then our soul will be able to maintain the mood and carry into the outer world what it has experienced in the worlds of spirit. That is part of the development of the theosophist. Thus we shall again come a step forward if we take such feelings with us and absorb with them the strengthening forces of the summer.

CPSIA information can be obtained at www.ICGtesting.com
Printed in the USA
LVOW04s2212220415

435733LV00031B/704/P